# ROBERT IRWIN

# WEALTH BUILDERS

## SIX "GET RICH QUICK" STRATEGIES THAT REALLY WORK

Franklin Watts    New York
1985    Toronto

Library of Congress Cataloging in Publication Data

Irwin, Robert, 1941–
Wealth builders.

Includes index.
1. Investments—Handbooks, manuals, etc. I. Title.
HG4527.I79  1985       332.6'78       84-25749
ISBN 0-531-09587-8

Copyright © 1985 by Robert Irwin
All rights reserved
Printed in the United States
6  5  4  3  2  1

This publication contains the author's opinion on the subject. It must be noted that neither the publisher nor the author is engaged in rendering investment, legal, tax, accounting, or similar professional services. While investment, legal, tax and accounting issues in this book have been checked with sources believed to be reliable, some material may be affected by changes in the laws or in the interpretations of such laws since the manuscript for this book was completed. Therefore, the accuracy and completeness of such information and the opinions based thereon are not and cannot be guaranteed. In addition, state or local tax laws or procedural rules may have a material impact on the recommendations made by the author, and the strategies outlined in this book may not necessarily be suitable in every case. If legal, accounting, tax, investment, or other expert advice is required, one should obtain the services of a competent practitioner. The publisher and author hereby specifically disclaim any liability for loss or risk incurred as a consequence of the advice or information presented in this book.

# CONTENTS

Preface
1

Introduction
3

**CHAPTER ONE**
Why Most Investors Don't
Become Millionaires
7

**CHAPTER TWO**
The Four Keys to
Building Your Wealth
21

**CHAPTER THREE**
Finding Your Best
Investment Opportunities
31

**CHAPTER FOUR**
Buying and Holding
Brand New Homes
39

**CONTENTS**

**CHAPTER FIVE**
Timed Bullion Risks
83

**CHAPTER SIX**
Ins and Outs of Rare Coins
115

**CHAPTER SEVEN**
Options for the Daring Investor
135

**CHAPTER EIGHT**
Opportunities in Tax Sales
151

**CHAPTER NINE**
The Penny Stock Boom
169

Conclusion
198

Index
200

# WEALTH BUILDERS

# PREFACE

If the best investment you've been able to make recently has been leaving your money in the bank or a money market fund, this book is for you!

When I was asked to write *Wealth Builders*, I emphasized that the book take a "common sense" approach to investing. I have seen too many investors who have lost their shirt in ridiculous schemes. There were to be no overleveraged tax shelters, no diamond plays, no real estate resales trying to cash in on yesterday's market. My idea was to come up with a book that would give the average person a half-dozen solid opportunities—investments that really work.

*Wealth Builders* is specifically attuned to the economic climate of the mid-1980s. It shows how to make an investment that works with—not against—interest rates and inflation. It explains which investments are high-risk and high-profit and which are low-risk and high-profit.

Miracles are not promised overnight, but the book presents the steps to follow in order to succeed. With these methods of investing, you don't need a lot of money, you need a lot of "smarts."

Anytime you invest your money, you risk losing it. Consequently, you should never invest anything until you've thoroughly researched the field and received a go-ahead from your personal financial advisor and your attorney.

## WEALTH BUILDERS

Because of the multitude and diversity of investment opportunities today, because of the sometimes irrational way that people can invest, and because of unforeseen circumstances that can turn winners to losers, **the author offers no guarantee or assurance of success with any of the investments, methods or techniques offered in this book.**

What this book does offer are the building blocks to wealth. My goal in writing it is to show you the path, not lead you down it. For the relatively small investment in this book, you can learn how to build your own road to financial fortune.

# INTRODUCTION

"I want to be a winner, but I'm a born loser!" The man was addressing the first meeting of the Future Millionaires' Investment Club,* to which I had been invited as a guest speaker. There were a little over a dozen people in the room and before it was my turn to speak, each in turn was standing and briefly describing his or her investment story.

The man continued, "My name is George, and I bought Washington State Power because I wanted *security*. You know what happened. They were the first utility company to default in anybody's memory. My bonds are worth nothing. I went for the safest investment I could think of . . . and I still lost! That's why I joined this investment club. I hope you all can help me get rich!"

He sat down amid a round of applause. Poor fellow, I thought. Perhaps the next speaker had better luck in investing.

The next person was a woman. "My name is Dorothy, but my yellow brick road led to disaster. A man told me that I could make a fortune buying houses for no down

---

* This was an informal group composed of friends and business associates, having no relation to the National Association of Investment Clubs or any other organization. All references to persons in this book are fictional and are used solely for the purpose of illustration.

—3—

payment. He even showed me how to buy them, including what to write into the sales contract.

"I took his advice and bought five, but they didn't go up in value. I had to put in nearly $1,500 of my own money *every month* just to keep them out of foreclosure. After two years I hadn't made a dime and I had spent $35,000. So I let them go back to the mortgage company. Now I've got five foreclosures against my name!"

There were sighs around the room. Then another woman stood up. "I must have met the same man as the last speaker! I'm Carrie, but I'm not carefree, not any more. The man told me I could get tax advantages and make my million by buying houses with only 10 percent down.

"My own house more than doubled in value during the seventies, so I figured he had to be right about investment houses today. I bought two and put $10,000 in each one. Sure I got a tax break, but that was eaten up by the negative cash flow on the properties. It has cost me $200 a month for the past three years to keep my houses. Now I've got over $25,000 in them and if I try to sell, after real estate commissions I'd be lucky to get out with $5,000.

"Buying with 10 percent down has been a disaster to me. I remember just a few years ago hearing a joke about how a good salesperson sold a million-dollar building for just $500 down. Maybe he did, but I bet that buyer is in foreclosure in today's real estate market."

After a few chuckles, a man stood up. "I'm George Golden but I've got no Midas touch," he said. "I'm just like these two ladies, only I lost my money investing in gold.

"The fellow I followed seemed to know everything about gold. He even assured me my investment would be protected in an underground vault. Only one day he com-

## INTRODUCTION

mitted suicide, and the next day when they opened the vault they found it was only filled with wooden bars painted to look like gold.

"I just don't know who to listen to," he said.

There followed two more people. One had lost money in diamonds, the other, again, in real estate.

Then a woman said, "I made the classic mistake. I bought stock when the market was going up, got ahead a little, then lost a bundle when the market dropped. I just didn't know when to stop. By the way, I'm Heather."

Finally it was my turn. I rose with some apprehension. I asked, "Has anyone in this room *ever* made any money by investing?"

I was surprised to see nearly everyone raise their hands. "But you all told horror stories about how you lost. Where did you make your money?" I pointed to Dorothy.

"I made it when I stuck my money in a money market fund."

George, Carrie, Heather, and the others nodded assent. One shouted out, "The only time I ever made money was when I left it in the bank. Every time I took it out, I lost!"

Carrie added, "Don't forget me. I made money on my own house, but of course that was back in the 1970s."

Others mumbled agreement and nodded.

"In other words," I said, "when it was in real estate before 1980 or what amounts to a savings account, such as a money market fund or in the bank, you made a little bit. But whenever you tried to take control of your investing, you lost?"

They looked around at each other and everyone seemed to be nodding agreement.

"But now you figure you'll never make your million

by putting your money in the bank, so you've joined an investment club to learn how to build wealth by investing on your own."

This time everyone was emphatically nodding assent and saying yes.

"OK," I said, "then the first thing we need to do is to see what mistakes you've been making in past investments. Then we can move on to see what you need to do to become a winner today."

# CHAPTER ONE

# WHY MOST INVESTORS DON'T BECOME MILLIONAIRES

I believe that every person in America wants to be a millionaire. The reason I believe this is because I've never met anyone who didn't. Any person I talk with for any length of time very soon expresses the desire to become wealthy. It must be our national obsession. The reason you're here, in fact, is that you want to become a millionaire. (I was addressing the Future Millionaires' Investment Club.)

Yet, there are very few millionaires. By the latest census there are only about half a million of them. That's less than a third of 1 percent of our whole population. It's a tiny, tiny group of people.

Why are there so few? Can it be that an economic structure is like a pyramid and there have to be millions and millions on the bottom to support a lucky few at the top?

If you believe that, think again. In some countries millionaires are the rule. A quarter of the population of oil rich Kuwait, for example, would probably qualify as millionaires. Even the poorest person there makes the equivalent of about $75,000 a year (including government benefits). And the country gets richer every day. You want the easy way to live among millionaires, arrange to be born in Kuwait!

There's no economic reason, however, why there can't be millionaires around every corner in this country, too. The country probably would be better off for it.

There's certainly no lack of opportunity. At any given time there are a thousand different ways that you and I can make money. In fact, it's hard to turn around without bumping into someone who's making bundles of cash.

But if it's economically possible and opportunity abounds, why aren't there more millionaires? If it's so easy to make money and so many people are doing it, why aren't there a hundred times more millionaires?

The reason is simple: *Most people lose $1.25 for each $1 they make by investing.* When it comes to earning a living, we all tend to get by. But when it comes to investing, most of us are walking catastrophes.

Look at yourselves. (I directed my attention to the people in the room.) Almost every time you invested, you lost. Unless it was in real estate in the 1970s (when prices were going up daily and it was virtually impossible to get a bad deal), the only time you made any money is when you stuck it in the bank or a money market fund.

Your personal investment careers have been the opposite of what you wanted. Instead of building success, you've built failure.

## THE PROBLEM

What's important to understand is that it doesn't have to be that way. It is possible to make money, bundles of money, starting with modest investments. It's even possible to make so much money that after a few years you can stop worrying about earning a living and retire to concentrate on your investments.

## WHY MOST INVESTORS DON'T BECOME MILLIONAIRES

But before that can happen, you first have to come to grips with what's causing you to lose on investments. In psychotherapy it's commonly said that when a patient finally understands that he or she has a problem, that person is more than halfway down the road to recovery.

In investing it's the same way. A lot of us don't feel that we have a problem. We blame bad luck on our wife or husband or our financial adviser or the president or the Federal Reserve Bank. We put the blame everywhere but where it really belongs, with us.

Here's a simple truth. In a society such as ours where opportunities to make money abound, if we can't invest successfully, *we* are doing something wrong. We ourselves are the problem. Before we can become part of the solution we must correct ourselves.

Of course, no investor is like another. My own investment weaknesses may not be yours. We each have our own distinct ways of holding ourselves back.

However, over the course of my own investing and by discussing this issue with others, both successful and not, I've discovered seven common reasons that people lose on their investments. I call these Loser's Reasoning.

I'm going to give you the seven, and I suggest you look closely to see if you are falling into any of their traps.

### LOSER'S REASONING 1: POSITIVE THINKING IS ALL YOU NEED

You know what positive thinking is. It's been promoted as the greatest thing since sliced bread. It asserts that if you believe you want to be rich, visualize it, think it, you'll soon find a way to be rich. "I will succeed because I be-

## WEALTH BUILDERS

lieve I will succeed." The mind is a powerful tool, according to this line of reasoning, and if you concentrate its power to move forward, you'll soon be a millionaire.

That's true, in part. But think about it. If positive thinking were *all* that was needed, why we really could do anything, couldn't we? Nothing would be impossible for us—not even, for example, flying without wings.

Just ask the man they fished out of San Francisco Bay who tried flying off the Golden Gate Bridge. He'll give you a hundred good reasons why positive thinking *alone* doesn't work.

I'm *for* positive thinking. I believe it is an essential ingredient in anyone's success. But I'm *against* the belief that *only* positive thinking is what's needed.

There have been so many books written and so many would-be messiahs have made their own fortunes preaching it, that I feel it's necessary to finally stand up and say, "Hold on!" Yes, to succeed you must have a positive approach. But you must also know exactly what you're doing.

An investor once said to me, "I have no reverse gear. I only go forward, and I go forward faster and faster."

That was right before he dumped $90,000 into a photo franchise. He didn't know anything about photography, and six months later he was broke.

He had a positive mind, but he also had an empty mind.

### LOSER'S REASONING 2:
### FOLLOW TODAY'S
### FINANCIAL HERO

I'm sure you know who a financial hero is. She can be the person who's on the radio or television telling you to buy

## WHY MOST INVESTORS DON'T BECOME MILLIONAIRES

real estate just as the market takes off. Or the fellow who writes a book predicting a crash just before it occurs. Because the individual predicted the event and then it happened, we conclude that he or she has got to have *hidden knowledge*.

Or the financial hero can be that person who gives a seminar and owns a big car and an impressive company and tells you that he can get you gold at discount or has insider's information on hot stocks or knows the perfect investment for you. Because this person has the giant company, the fancy car, maybe even the diamond stickpin, because this fellow has all the accoutrements of success, he must be successful, hence he must have hidden knowledge.

Let me explode a few myths. People are *always* predicting every market is going to go up or go down or crash. Some of them have to be right some of the time. It doesn't make them financial geniuses; it doesn't mean they have hidden knowledge. It just means they were lucky, once.

And just because a person exhibits wealth in a flashy way, doesn't mean he or she *is* wealthy or even knows how to make money by investing. That person may have all his money tied up in his jewelry and car. The only way that person may really know how to make money is by giving seminars on investing to others who also don't know how.

If you need further proof, ask yourself this: What's the lifespan of a financial hero? If you think back I'm sure you'll discover it's rarely more than two years. Think about it. Who is today's guru? Was he or she around five years ago? One year ago? Wasn't there a different guru two years ago? Wasn't there yet another financial hero four years ago? And yet others going back at intervals of about every two years?

Financial heroes don't last long in our world. The reason is that whatever they happen to be promoting that appears successful at the moment, is quickly passed by changing times.

Real financial gurus, those who know how to make big money, rarely share their knowledge and even more rarely make a splashy appearance. They prefer that you *don't* know who they are! Chances are you'll *never* hear the real expert who makes a bundle on the market giving an investment seminar.

It's one of the truths of the business world that those who have found a way to make big money rarely share their knowledge with anyone else (they're too busy making money for themselves). Here are some others. No one *ever* sells gold at discount. True insiders *never* tell anyone else *all* that they know. Even in this book, while I'm going to give you a strategy and plan that may make you successful, I'm not going to tell you exactly which option or coin or penny stock or other investment I'm buying or you should buy. My goal is to point out the path, not lead you down it.

Remember, today's financial heroes don't really lead, they follow. They just tell us what we want to hear.

### LOSER'S REASONING 3: YOU CAN DUPLICATE SOMEONE ELSE'S INVESTMENT SUCCESS

This rule always reminds me of the old pyramid game, which becomes popular about every thirty years. You get two people to "invest" a thousand dollars with you. They get four people to invest a thousand with them. Those in turn get eight people to invest a thousand with them, and on and on.

The first few layers of people do quadruple or more their money. But eventually we run out of fools near the bottom of the pyramid and the whole thing collapses. The vast majority of "investors" are near the bottom. By trying to duplicate someone else's success, they end up being the bigger fool and losing.

You can't duplicate another person's success. If you try, all you'll accomplish is to duplicate your own previous failure.

There's more than enough opportunity around for you to discover your own success.

## LOSER'S REASONING 4: DON'T WASTE TIME STUDYING AN INVESTMENT; GET IN WHILE IT'S HOT

This follows from Loser's Reasoning 2. Real estate is hot, gold is hot, stocks are hot, something else is hot. We see others making money in one field or another and think it's hot, so we plow our money in behind.

One of the oldest rules of investing is, "When the public gets in, it's time to get out."

I spent nearly fifteen years writing about rare coin investments. I've talked with thousands of people and I've been an adviser for *COINage*, the world's largest-circulation coin magazine.

Yet in all that time I've met only a handful of investors who followed the cardinal rule of that field: "Buy the book before the coin."

**WEALTH BUILDERS**

What it means is that you can't hope to succeed in coin investing—or anything else—until you understand the market you're in.

Most investors get into an investment because they've heard a rumor that it's hot. Sometimes the rumor is indeed true, and investing in the field may be a wise decision. But until you've studied the field and the particular investment, you won't know the three necessary facts that any investor must know to succeed:

1. What do I buy?
2. When do I get in?
3. When do I get out?

If instead of rushing in, an investor would take the relatively short time required to differentiate top quality from junk, would learn about a field's and an investment's one-year, five-year, ten-year, and fifty-year performance background, would study the reasons an investment is going up, then success might be assured.

Unfortunately, most investors simply hear that some people are making money in one area or another and jump in. Even if they're right about the field and they make some money, they usually still lose because they don't know enough to get out in time.

I knew an investor who made a fortune when silver shot up in value back in 1980. He bought futures contracts at $35 an ounce. For every dollar silver when up in price, he made $5,000 due to leverage.

Within a few weeks the price of silver shot up to nearly $50 dollars an ounce. He had made $75,000 in days!

"Sell," I told him.

"Are you crazy?" he shouted at me. "It'll hit $100 before the month's out!"

## WHY MOST INVESTORS DON'T BECOME MILLIONAIRES

Silver moved again quickly. It shot back down to $25. It shot down so fast, in fact, that he was locked into his futures contracts and couldn't sell! He lost every penny he made and more.

"Why didn't you tell me to sell when it was at $50?" he moaned.

"I was sure I had," I replied.

He knew what to buy and when to buy. But he lacked the third vital ingredient that learning about the field would have given him—knowing when to get out.

If he had studied the history and the market for silver he would have known that it couldn't possibly sustain a $50 price at the time. It had to fall.

Most investors don't spend even one day really studying the investment they make. Is it any wonder that either they don't make any money or, if they do make some, frequently lose what they made and more?

### LOSER'S REASONING 5: WAIT FOR JUST THE RIGHT INVESTMENT

What's wrong with that? You certainly wouldn't want to put your money in the wrong investment, would you? It makes sense to wait.

There's an old story I remember from grammar school that may be able to explain the problem here. A student wanted very much to receive the praise of his teacher and the admiration of his friends by raising his hand in class and giving the correct answer to a teacher's question.

There were plenty of opportunities. The trouble was that the questions the teacher was asking were hard. The student frequently thought he knew the answer, but he wasn't a hundred percent sure. One or two other students would always raise their hands. Sometimes they'd be wrong, but sometimes they'd be right and then they'd get the praise and admiration that our friend wanted.

So he waited and waited until the teacher finally asked a question that he was absolutely sure he knew the answer to, and he raised his hand. Only when he looked around, he saw that *everyone* else in the class had also raised their hand. The teacher picked another person.

The point is that if you wait for the sure bet, the only thing you're sure to get is lost in the crowd.

It's important to be *in the market*. This simply means that you are active. You occasionally buy and sell. Thus when a good deal comes along, you can recognize it and you feel comfortable taking a chance.

A corollary of this has to do with *being ready*. As we all know, timing is vital to success. Ideally we want to get our resources ready to act at a moment's notice.

However, some of us make the mistake of thinking that just because we are finally ready, the market is too. The fact is that good investments come and go. They aren't always available. One of the worst things I've seen people do is work hard to get some capital together and then immediately invest it in the first thing that comes along.

The chances of their finding a terrific investment just at the precise moment they get their money together are almost nil. They'd be far better off sticking that money in the bank.

You can't wish up a great investment opportunity. It's either there or it isn't. If you wait for the perfect investment, you'll be crowded out. But if you have the money and spend it when the investment isn't worthwhile, you'll lose too.

## WHY MOST INVESTORS DON'T BECOME MILLIONAIRES

The market doesn't give a hoot or a holler whether or not you're ready to invest. When the opportunity's there, it's there. Either you're in the market, see it, and grab for it, or you lose out.

### LOSER'S REASONING 6A: LOSING MONEY IS THE WORST THING THAT CAN HAPPEN TO ME

I've lost money in stocks, in real estate, in options and in other areas. But I've always made more than I've lost. The occasional loss didn't deter me. What's more important, the fear of losing didn't keep me from investing.

This is closely related to Loser's Reasoning 5. The fear of losing can not only keep you waiting for just the right investment, it can keep you from ever investing.

Some of the great achievers in our world were losers at one time or another. Edison at first went broke. So did Walt Disney and President Grant. You can't hope to succeed every time. You can hope only to succeed eventually.

It's all right to lose money. I'll repeat that in case you missed it. *It's all right to lose money!* Of course it's better to make it. The point is that we can't allow an occasional loss to paralyze us. Like the person who falls off a horse, we must get up, get on, and ride again, or give up forever.

In investing as in most fields, *persistence* pays off.

### LOSER'S REASONING 6B: I DON'T CARE IF I LOSE!

This is the opposite case to 6A, that is, the person who has no fear at all. I call these people "players."

Players play the stock market or play the real estate market or play the commodities market. These people aren't interested in becoming millionaires. They're only interested in playing a game.

Remember the story of the student in the classroom? Well, he had a classmate who wasn't a bit like him. His classmate was a girl who *always* raised her hand. Sometimes she knew the answer, but most of the time she didn't. It didn't make any difference. Every time the teacher asked a question, her hand was up.

It got so bad that finally the teacher called her to the front of the room and asked her privately, "Kathleen, why are you always raising your hand even when you don't know the answer?"

She replied, "Because it's so much fun!"

When you win at an investment, you're going to think it's great fun. But I've never met an investor who enjoyed losing. You have to decide what your goal will be. Do you want to play, or do you want to win?

## LOSER'S REASONING 7: ALWAYS BELIEVE A SELLER

There is one rule that is probably the single most important for success. This rule is ultimately more important than being positive or having money or outguessing the market. Can you guess what the rule is?

It's simply two words, *"Ask why."*

*Why* is there such a good deal today in a particular stock? *Why* is this investment house so cheap? *Why* are the silver dollars underpriced?

## WHY MOST INVESTORS DON'T BECOME MILLIONAIRES

P. T. Barnum is reputed to have said, "There's a sucker born every minute." That has become the motto of the millions of sellers who are waiting to give you "the world's greatest deal!"

Anytime we consider buying anything we must first ask ourselves, "Why is it for sale? Why is it offered at this price? Why to me?"

I met a person not long ago who bought "discounted gold."

"What's that?" I asked.

"It was a wonderful opportunity," he explained. "This company which manufactures electronic equipment uses gold at electrical contact points. Only they overbought and had to quickly liquidate their stock. They offered it to me for 25 percent off to get rid of it fast. How could I refuse?"

"You should have," I observed. "Gold is international currency. Nobody offers to sell you gold at discount any more than they would offer to sell you 'surplus' paper dollars at discount."

He looked at me in disbelief and said he already had the bars. I suggested he have them assayed.

It turned out that the gold was mixed with copper and other metals in an alloy. It was only 50 percent gold. His great deal turned out to be a bad bargain.

Anytime anyone wants to sell you anything, question his or her motives. You can be sure that the seller will gain something on the sale (else he or she wouldn't sell). Find out what that gain is, and you'll know whether or not you should buy.

In a good deal both buyer and seller understand what benefits each is getting. They both understand the other's motivation.

**WEALTH BUILDERS**

In a bad deal, only the seller knows the buyer's motivation. The surest way I know of to lose money in investing is to overlook the seller's motivation and instead let greed be your guide.

I turned to the audience. "Did you find yourself in any of these Loser's Reasonings?" I asked.

There were nods from various places around the room.

"Don't criticize yourself," I said. At one time or another we *all* fall into those traps. The important thing is that we realize that *we* can be our own worst enemy. It's not our spouse or the Fed or the president or our financial adviser who's causing our investment downfall. We have to look closer for the real problem.

Now let's look at some solutions. Let's consider some positive keys that most successful investors use to unlock the doors to wealth.

# CHAPTER TWO

# THE FOUR KEYS TO BUILDING YOUR WEALTH

While there are at least seven reasons why people lose money in investing, as we saw in the last chapter, I believe that there are only four keys to success. (I was addressing the Future Millionaires' Investment Club. I had just described seven reasons that could have caused them to fail in earlier investing. Now we were considering how to succeed.)

It's like the muscles in our face, I explained to them. It takes something like a hundred muscles to make a frown. But it takes only about twenty-five to smile. It takes a lot of effort to fail, but success can be so much easier.

I have never found anyone who made a fortune by investing who did not know these four keys and who did not use them constantly. It didn't make any difference whether that person was an entrepreneur opening a business or a stock purchaser. It doesn't matter if you're investing in real estate or coins. *Without these four keys you cannot succeed.* With them you will acquire wealth.

## SUCCESS KEY 1: YOU MAKE YOUR OWN LUCK

Mathematics teaches us that there is no such thing as luck. It doesn't exist. There are only probabilities.

# WEALTH BUILDERS

Yet, most people fervently believe in luck. I've seen this most clearly in the game of poker. Most people believe that poker, which is seeing renewed popularity in this country today, is a game of luck. The winner is the luckiest player.

However, as any good poker player will tell you, nothing could be further from the truth. Poker is not a game of luck, but rather a game of skill and money management (much like investing).

Set any seven players down in a real poker game, one in which you can't leave the table until either you've lost all your money or won everyone else's, and the winner will be the most skillful player and best money manager.

In the short run, over a few hours, one player or another may get a "lucky streak" when the cards seem to go his or her way. But over the long haul the good cards and bad cards average out and it's the player who knows the odds and can manage money best who wins.

(If you don't believe me, ask a good poker player how "lucky" he has to be to bet on drawing a fifth card to an inside straight. He'll tell you exactly, "It's a sucker's bet." The good player isn't concerned about luck, he's concerned about probabilities.)

In investing it's much the same way. Most people think that successful investors are lucky. Again, nothing could be further from the truth. Yes, certainly, over the short term a person might fall into a terrific deal.

But over the long haul, the millionaires are the ones who are skillful with what investment opportunities come their way and with managing the money they have. In other words, if you are in the market you will come across both good investments and bad ones. It's your skill and how you

## THE FOUR KEYS TO BUILDING YOUR WEALTH

handle your resources that will determine if you make a bundle.

Investors who are successful often scoff at luck. The most commonly heard statement among them is that a successful person makes his or her own luck.

## SUCCESS KEY 2:
## YOU PAY YOUR DUES

In the investment world, the opportunities out there aren't stacked either for you or against you. Nobody is trying to make you win or make you lose. You do it all on your own.

Chances are that when you first begin investing, you will have modest opportunities. These are ones where you probably won't make a lot of money, but you probaby won't lose very much either.

As you succeed in these early investments, however, they will lead you to increasingly complex investments which involve ever bigger amounts of money, where the opportunity to win or lose is for ever higher stakes.

When you finally get into really big money, you'll be making decisions on deals involving hundreds of thousands, perhaps millions of dollars.

The point to see, however, is that to get to the top, you have to start near the bottom. You have to begin with modest deals and *build on the knowledge and experience you gain.*

This is obvious if you have only a small amount of money to start with. But starting near the bottom is important for another reason. It allows you to learn about the market without a lot of pressure. You can make your errors early while the stakes are still low. There are few things sadder than seeing a man or woman jump into a market with $100,000 and quickly lose it all simply because they never paid their dues; the person never learned how to operate in that market.

When you start low you gain at least three basic building blocks that you need for successful investing:

    **1.** You learn about the market you are in. It won't do you any good to spend a year abstractly studying stocks at a university. You can learn more in one day by buying a stock. It's when you put up your own money and enter a market that you really learn about it.

    **2.** You learn about yourself. You see how you feel when you win a few dollars or lose a few. You see how long you are willing to wait for a win. You come to understand yourself as a conservative investor or a plunger.

    **3.** You learn the techniques of investing in the market. If, for example, it's gold, you learn about dealers and what to expect from them. You learn about pricing, about quality, about standards. In other markets you learn their parameters.

These are building blocks that you must have underneath you in order to succeed in investing. It's far better that you get them at a level where the stakes are low, than get them when you're pushing around $100,000 chips. When I say, "You pay your dues," I mean you've gone through the learning process of starting off small and building on the blocks of knowledge that you've learned so that when it

# THE FOUR KEYS TO
# BUILDING YOUR WEALTH

comes time to invest $700,000 of your own money, you have the background to make the winning decision.

## SUCCESS KEY 3:
## MOVE WITH THE TIMES

I consider this a vital key to success (one we'll talk more about in the next chapter).

If you are going to have any hope of success, you must understand that investments are like the tide—they ebb and flow.

I'm sure you've had the experience of building sand castles. I can remember once, as a child, I and several other children built a beautiful castle near the water's edge. We began in the morning when the tide was receding. How easy it was to build. As the waves moved out of our way, we added walls, rooms and towers. But then, by late afternoon, the tide changed direction.

Walls that had easily held the water before, now were quickly washed away. As the tide came in, our castle crumpled no matter how fast we tried to rebuild it.

I remember one boy who laid his body down in front of the castle hoping to keep the waves from taking it. It worked for a short time, but soon the entire portion of beach we were on was under water and our castle was gone.

Investments are like that. When we are investing with the flow, we can't seem to lose. Yet, when the tide turns, it seems like we can't win. The idea, of course, is never to invest against the tide.

Yet many, many people do buck the trend. We win a few times in silver, hence, we are commited forever after to investing in silver. Even when the tide in silver is running against us, we are still out there trying to turn a deal. The result is we get washed away.

No investments are always winners. All investments have good times and bad times.

If you bought residential real estate in the 1960s, chances are you didn't make much, if any, money. The tide wasn't with you. However, if you bought and sold in the 1970s the tide was rolling your way and you made a bundle.

If you bought gold and silver between 1978 and early 1981, you probably did very well. Precious metals were flowing. But, if you bought before or after, you were bucking the tide and probably lost.

If you bought stocks in 1981 and 1982, by 1983 you were a winner. If you held into early 1984, the tide had turned and you probably were a loser.

If you speculated in foreign currency in 1977, by 1978 and 1979 you were probably well on your way to becoming a millionaire. If you kept on buying foreign currency in 1979 or 1984, you were on your way to the poorhouse.

The list goes on and on. It holds true for *all* investments and, in truth, for life in general. Even in the Bible it's written, "To every thing there is a season, and a time to every purpose under the heaven." (Ecclesiastes 3, 1.) Timing is everything.

You want to be *in* real estate when it's moving up and *out* of real estate when it's going down or stagnating. You want to be *in* stocks as the market moves up and *out* of stocks when it moves down. *In* gold, silver, diamonds, commodities, etc., when they are moving up, *out* when they are moving down. (The only area you can be in all the time is futures contracts or options, where you can bet either way. We'll say more about this in a later chapter.)

## THE FOUR KEYS TO
## BUILDING YOUR WEALTH

There are two lessons to be learned here, both of which are valid:
1. Every investment has a good time and a bad. No investment is *always* good or *always* bad.
2. You can't just stick to one investment or one field. You can't just be in real estate or stocks or gold. To win you must move from field to field taking advantage of the flow.

### SUCCESS KEY 4:
### YOU MUST
### HAVE A WRITTEN PLAN

Can you imagine this conversation occurring in the Defense Department sometime in 1942 during World War II?

*Scientist:* "We're going to build a bomb that will end this war!"
*Politician:* "Anything that will shorten the war will be wonderful. How long before it will be ready?"
*Scientist:* "That's hard to say."
*Politician:* "Well, what kind of a bomb will it be?"
*Scientist:* "I don't really know."
*Politician (in exasperation):* "Well, how are you going to build it?"
*Scientist:* "We don't really know. We just keep hoping."

If this had really happened, do you think the atomic bomb would ever have been developed?

The same holds true with investments. You can succeed in even your most incredible goals, but only if you have a workable plan.

What then, is a workable plan?

A workable plan has at least three parts. The first part is a time frame. A time frame breaks up the future into blocks of time with goals at the end of each block.

## Time Goals

Almost all the successful people in history have had a time frame. It was often said about Jack Kennedy that he determined that by the time he was forty-five, he was going to be president. (He beat his goal by two years.) Winston Churchill, Albert Camus (the French writer/philosopher), even Julius Caesar all had time goals.

In investing, a time goal is something like the following:

> I agree that within five years I will have made $250,000 by investing.
>
> Within two years I will have made $50,000.
>
> Within the next ninety days I will make $1,000.

Those are time goals. Their purpose is to get us to commit ourselves to achieving a particular task. They are both long-term (five years out) and short-term (ninety days out). A good time frame will be built so that the short-term goals naturally lead us to achieving the longer ones.

## In Writing

The second part of a workable plan is commitment. Once we have time goals, we must commit ourselves to achieving them. We accomplish this by *writing them down*.

## THE FOUR KEYS TO BUILDING YOUR WEALTH

An architect doesn't commit her plan for a building to memory. She writes it down. A boat builder does the same. So too does anyone who wants a plan to succeed.

If we simply keep our time goals in our mind, it's too easy to change our time frame. If we don't achieve our goal in ninety days, it's oh so easy to move it back another ninety. If we don't achieve our five-year goal, we can take ten. Who's to know we failed?

But once it's written down (in ink), we can't change it. We can only succeed or fail (and we'll know if we fail!). It's the drive to succeed and the need not to fail that often pushes us into making our fortune.

### Skill

The last part of any workable plan is having the skill to pull it off. In investing having the skill means you must know the three items mentioned in the last chapter:

1. In what will you invest?
2. When will you get in?
3. When will you get out?

Skill means learning about the investment area, getting your feet wet (being in the market), taking advantage of trends (as in Success Key 3 above) and planning your escape.

Skill, a time frame and a written plan frame are what you need to succeed. With them, you simply won't dare lose!

### THE FOUR KEYS

These then are the four keys that every successful investor knows:

**WEALTH BUILDERS**

1. Make your own luck.
2. Pay your dues.
3. Move with the times.
4. Have a written plan with a time frame.

I turned to the audience and asked for their reactions.
"You're right." Dorothy said.
"Yes, you are," agreed George. "But where's the meat? I agree with you, but where do I go from here?"
There was assent from around the room.
"Fine," I said, "let's look at what's happening in specific investments today and go out there and make some money!"

# CHAPTER THREE

# FINDING YOUR BEST INVESTMENT OPPORTUNITIES

"What's the best investment out there?"

There were mumbles from around the room as the members of the Future Millionaires' Investment Club tossed the question around between themselves. "Penny stocks," someone called. "Condo conversions," came another reply. "Palladium," came yet another.

"What's palladium?" someone asked. "It's like gold, only cheaper," came the reply.

"Hold on," I told them. "The answer is that there is no one 'best' investment. Rather, a good investment is often a function of *when* we invest."

### THE ONLY TWO "SURE BET" INVESTMENTS SINCE WORLD WAR II

I went on to explain that since World War II there have only been two times when what to invest in was obvious to everyone. The first time had been in the 1950s. At that time the stock market had surged upward at a steady pace for year after year. You didn't have to be smart or careful. All you had to do was simply put your money into stocks and watch it grow rapidly.

## WEALTH BUILDERS

(The reason stocks had boomed was because American businesses were expanding to accommodate both enormous consumer demand at home and a blossoming world market. Of course, since the mid-1960s these growth conditions have not existed and, hence, since then we haven't been able to throw our money at Wall Street and get rich.)

## THROWING MONEY AT REAL ESTATE

The second time when successful investing was obvious was in the late 1970s. During this period real estate was soaring in value. Many homes tripled in price over a five-year period. Some apartment buildings quadrupled in value. You didn't have to be careful or clever in the Seventies either. All you had to do was throw your money into real estate to get rich.

(The reason that real estate boomed was twofold. First it was because there was plentiful, low-interest-rate financing, which made it easy to make high-leverage deals—this at the same time that high inflation was boosting the cost of everything around us. The second cause of the real estate boom was the tax advantages that real estate offers, namely the ability to deduct interest on the mortgage, local taxes, and—in the case of investment property—depreciation from income taxes. However, since 1980 few low-interest-rate mortgages have been available, and over the course of the next few years some of the tax advantages of real estate are quite likely to be stripped away. Hence, after 1980 real estate no longer has been the easy winner it was in the 1970s.)

**FINDING YOUR BEST
INVESTMENT OPPORTUNITIES**

## MORE THAN ONE WINNER

That doesn't mean, however, that there aren't enormous opportunities today. It just means that there isn't just one area that's an obvious winner. Rather, there are many areas.

"But, how do we know which investment field is going to win?" It was George asking the question. He had invested in a "sure bet," and had lost everything.

"That's the $64 question." I replied. "But there is a way to know."

## HOW TO KNOW WHICH
## FIELD TO INVEST IN

There are factors which determine which field will do well and which won't, I explained. I call them "challenges" because they challenge investments.

In the 1970s the challenge was *productivity*.

During that decade the American worker produced ever less for ever more money. Our worker's "productivity," or ability to create a product for a given reward, grew smaller and smaller. Other countries were outproducing us, and we were paying the penalty in the form of a dollar which declined in value relative to other currency.

Our government, in the form of the Federal Reserve Bank, clung to an outmoded policy born of the Great Depression which said, "Prosperity comes about when interest rates are low." It kept interest rates low in the face of decreasing productivity, which resulted in an enormous increase in the money supply and, ultimately, in soaring inflation. It was high inflation coupled with low interest rates, in fact, that made investment in real estate so profitable during the 1970s.

## THE NEW CHALLENGE IS LIQUIDITY

That changed when we entered the 1980s. A new Federal Reserve policy of reduced monetary growth (even if it resulted in high interest rates) took effect. The country was plunged into a deep recession. Workers were forced to accept less and to work more.

During the early 1980s for the first time since the 1950s and early 1960s, the productivity of American workers actually *grew!* The challenge of productivity had been met and beaten, at least momentarily.

But a new challenge was raising its head. In 1981 the Reagan administration drastically cut taxes at the same time as it (although unwillingly) increased the federal budget due to increased defense spending. The result, as we all know, was an enormously increased *federal deficit.* The size of the deficit can perhaps best be judged by the interest payments on it. When President Reagan took office it took roughly $50 billion annually to pay the interest on the national debt. Four years later that interest payment had risen to roughly $150 billion, and that was during a time of very modest inflation. (If we project that increase out into the future, by about 1999 it will take *all* of the country's taxed income just to pay the interest on the debt, leaving nothing on which to run the country!)

## HOW THE FEDERAL DEFICIT CREATED OUR PERSONAL CHALLENGE

Most of us have yawned when we have heard about the national debt. "So what?" is a common comment. "How does it affect me?"

## FINDING YOUR BEST INVESTMENT OPPORTUNITIES

The answer is that as investors it affects us dramatically. The size of our national debt actually helps us determine which investments over the next few years will be profitable and which won't.

### HOW THE DEFICIT AFFECTS LIQUIDITY

Put simply, the government borrows to pay the national debt. Its borrowing competes with that of private business (and of us with our Mastercards and Visas). The competition forces interest rates (which are the price of money) to rise.

Who can afford high rates? First of all, the government. The federal government can pay any rate, so it takes all it needs of the available money.

Next, there are businesses. They often must borrow to survive, hence, they pay the high rates (and sometimes are driven into bankruptcy because of their interest payments!).

Finally, there's you and I. When the rates get too high, we don't borrow. We put off buying that house or car or other item because we can't afford the interest rate on the loan we need to get.

It takes a while to see the relationship, but it's there. High deficits result in a money shortage. And the result of this, ultimately, is an economic blowout which results in a new recession.

### LIQUIDITY—THE CHALLENGE

The challenge for this decade, therefore, has become liquidity. How to get and manage cash.

Liquidity in everyday usage for you and me translates into how we deal with (usually) high interest rates. Last decade it was how we dealt with inflation. This decade we not only have to watch out for inflation, but high interest rates as well.

Because of the high government deficits, the liquidity challenge will undoubtedly translate into a seesaw economy during which at different times we can expect to see the following:

High inflation, high interest rates
Lower inflation, high interest rates
Lower inflation, lower interest rates
High inflation, lower interest rates (for brief periods)

Any investor who's going to win during this decade *must* take into account the fact that inflation and interest rates will be rising *and* falling continuously over the next several years. If we bet on inflation or interest rates *going only one way*, we'll lose. We can no longer count on ever higher inflation or on steady interest rates that way we could in the 1970s.

To win today, therefore, we must tailor our investments to the time. We must make ourselves "liquid investors." We must be able to move in and out of appropriate markets.

"Right!" It was George again in the audience. "Now you're getting to it. Which ones are the *appropriate* investments? Where exactly do we stick our money to win?"

We'll get to that soon enough, I told him. But just remember, what we're stressing here is that the answer to finding the right investment for this decade is to be able to get *in* and *out* of many different things *at the right time*.

## FINDING YOUR BEST
## INVESTMENT OPPORTUNITIES

## THE RIGHT INVESTMENTS
## FOR THE DECADE

There are many, many different investments. But I'm going to take six which I think are the best. We'll look at each one of these separately in terms of the liquidity challenge. The six are:

> Residential real estate
> Gold/silver/other bullion
> Rare coins
> Tax sales
> Options
> Penny stocks

## NO SURE BETS

As I noted earlier in this chapter, the only sure investment bets in the last fifty years were stocks in the 1950s and real estate in the late 1970s. Those times are both gone. Hence, there is no guarantee that investing in any of the above areas will be successful. This is particularly the case in this decade since *timing* is more important than ever.

Nevertheless, we can never win unless we are willing to take a chance on losing.

## BUYING AND HOLDING BRAND NEW HOMES

### RISK
Medium (if purchased correctly)

### WHEN TO BUY
Inflation—low, medium, or high
Interest rates—low to medium

### WHEN TO SELL
Inflation—medium to high
Interest rates—low to medium

### HOLDING PERIOD
Except for fixer-uppers, very long term
—ten years

### CASH REQUIRED
$10,000 (possible with little cash)

### PROFIT POTENTIAL
Enormous, a million dollars in equity
often possible over long term

### SKILL REQUIRED
Minimal (good common sense is essential)

### EFFORT REQUIRED
Should be done part-time

### MAJOR DIFFICULTY
Management of rented property

### PROBLEMS
Potential tax law change disallowing
interest deduction

# CHAPTER FOUR

## BUYING AND HOLDING BRAND NEW HOMES

> *Real estate is
> the poor man's road to wealth.*
>
> John Jacob Astor

"For the last ten years, anyone who wanted to get started on the road to wealth began by purchasing a rental house."

I was talking with Dorothy and Carrie of the Future Millionaires' Investment Club. They had determined to make their fortunes in real estate and agreed to work with me in the field over a few months to come up with good investment property.

"But," Dorothy protested, "the last time out I bought three houses and for nothing down. Only instead of making money, I've lost $15,000 and the houses!"

"You can add my experience to hers," said Carrie. "I bought two houses with only 10 percent down. I've invested $25,000 but within only two years my real equity is only $5,000. I'd hardly call that the road to riches!"

I tried to calm them. I pointed out that times change. What was true last year isn't necessarily true today. I pointed out that it was still possible to do well in residential real estate, but the rules of the game had changed.

WEALTH BUILDERS

## YESTERDAY'S RULES

When you bought your homes, I told them, you were playing the appreciation game. The appreciation game only has one rule. You tie up ownership in a house for as little of your money as possible. Then you wait for appreciation to move the price up until you can sell for a big profit.

There's nothing simpler than the appreciation game, when it works. But there has to be high inflation and low mortgage interest rates for it to work. Between 1982 and 1985 we had neither.

"I don't understand," commented Dorothy. "I bought for nothing down—how could I lose?"

"You lost,' I explained, "because you confused high-leverage financing with a sound investment. Let me tell you a little story that helps to illustrate this."

Once there was a farmer who became modestly successful in raising pigs for market. There wasn't a great deal of money in it, but it provided him with a consistent and adequate income.

He worked hard for several years; then one day he noticed that the middleman he sold his pigs to was making far more money than he. In fact while our farmer was just getting by, the middleman was getting rich.

"How can this be?" the farmer asked himself. "I'm breeding the pigs, paying for the feed, raising them to maturity, even slaughtering them; yet I'm only getting by, while the man I sell them to is making a fortune."

Finally the farmer asked the middleman his secret. At first he refused to say, but when the farmer pressed him, he replied, "All right, I tell you since I'm ready to retire anyhow and it won't make any difference."

"I don't care about pigs. I only care about prices. You

—40—

## BUYING AND HOLDING BRAND NEW HOMES

come to me after raising a pig and offer it for $50. I look around and I know that there's a big demand for pork these days. I know that I can quickly resell it for $55 to a store. So I buy your pig and turn it around, making a $5 profit. That's how I do it."

"But," protested the farmer, "you make only $5 on a pig. When I sell it to you I make $10 profit on each pig. I make twice the profit that you do, yet you're wealthy and I'm not. How can that be?"

The middleman laughed. "How many pigs a year can you raise?"

The farmer calculated, then answered, "300, maybe 350 in a good year."

"All right, then there's your answer," replied the middleman. "The most profit you can hope to make is $10 each on 350 pigs or $3,500. I, on the other hand, buy from you and nineteen other farmers. I make only $5 per pig but I buy and sell 7,000 pigs. While you're slaving to make your $3,500, I'm making $35,000 . . . and I never even get my hands dirty!"

The farmer was aghast. He went home and decided that he was in the wrong business. He immediately got out of raising pigs and began buying and selling them just as the middleman had. He very quickly began making loads of money.

Carrie shook her head. "I don't get it. We've done just what you described. We didn't raise pigs, of course, but we did tie up houses at one price hoping to sell higher. Yet unlike the middleman or the farmer in your story, we didn't make any money!"

I went on to explain that the story was not finished. At *first* the farmer did well because the market for pork bellies was going up. But then, the market turned down.

—41—

Our farmer suddenly found he was stuck with hundreds of pigs he had bought for $50 and he couldn't sell them unless he took a loss.

He began to tear out his hair. The pigs were already slaughtered. If he didn't sell them, he had to keep them in storage, which added to his costs. Very quickly he lost not only all the money he had previously made, but lots more besides.

After it was all over and our farmer got rid of his last pork belly at a loss, he went back to see the old middleman again. "What happened?" he asked. "I did exactly the same as you, only while you've retired with a fortune, I've gone broke."

The middleman laughed but was sympathetic. He replied, "To be a successful middleman you not only have to buy and sell; you also have to know when to get out of the market."

## BUYING AND QUICKLY RESELLING WORKS ONLY WHEN APPRECIATION IS HIGH

When I finished the story, Dorothy and Carrie looked at each other and nodded.

The plain fact, I explained, was that between about 1974 and 1980 the real estate market exploded in value. Housing prices nearly tripled. It was a time when being a middleman made sense. The way to get rich was to buy as many houses as you could for as little of your own money as possible.

In other words, tie up lots of property; then simply wait until inflation drove prices higher and sell for a profit. The more houses you could tie up, the more money you

## BUYING AND HOLDING BRAND NEW HOMES

could make. Buying for nothing down or only a little down made sense.

"In other words," said Dorothy, "you're saying that the strategy we used was geared strictly to a time of rapid price appreciation. But now times have changed?"

I nodded.

## REAL ESTATE DOES NOT ALWAYS GO UP FAST IN VALUE

"But real estate has always gone up in value," exclaimed Carrie. "It's still going up. Times really haven't changed."

That, I explained, simply wasn't so. I told them that I had heard promoters make the statement that real estate only goes up in value. The *truth*, however, is that while over the past fifty years real estate has gone up in value almost every year, in the vast majority of years the increase was very modest, often only a few hundred dollars.

The *problem* is that most recent investors in real estate don't have a long enough memory of the field. You have to go back further than the mid-1970s to get a true perspective. I explained my own recollections of selling real estate back in the 1950s. Yes, prices did go up every year, but only about $150 a house! In those days investors almost never bought to quickly resell. We bought mainly for two reasons. We bought (1) to simply hold for twenty or thirty years, having the tenants slowly pay off the mortgage and thereby build our equity for us. We also bought (2) to get a fixer-upper, refurbish it, and then sell for a profit. In the 1950s and 1960s real estate investors were less middlemen than producers. We refurbished or we bought to provide rentals over a long term.

It wasn't until the mid-1970s that anybody bought

houses hoping to turn them over for a profit in less than six months. It wasn't until then that *quick* middleman profits were possible. That was unheard of in the previous decades except in a few boom areas.

In the days before the 1970s real estate boom, you bought and refurbished or held. During the boom things were different and being a middleman paid off. But now, once again to make a profit in real estate you have to be a producer. Things have come full circle.

"It makes sense to me," Dorothy said. "But I don't see how Carrie or I can take advantage of the way things are today. It was simple before; now it seems complex."

I explained to them that things seem hard only when we don't understand them. In many respects making money in real estate today is simpler than it was five years ago. It's just that it's different. To understand how profits can be made now, we first need to really understand what today's conditions mean to us as investors.

### INTEREST RATES AND REAL ESTATE

Mortgage rates directly determine the *volume of sales* of real estate. Mortgage rates are the lifeblood of real estate. When rates are high, buyers can't or won't qualify for mortgages, sales volume plummets, and real estate prices level off and decline. When they are low, it's easy for buyers to get financing, sales volume shoots up, and real estate comes back to life.

Interest rates on mortgages climbed steadily after the Great Depression. Back in the 1940s rates were in the 3 to 5 percent range. By the 1950s we hit highs in the 8 to 9 percent area, but quickly dropped back down to 6 percent.

## BUYING AND HOLDING BRAND NEW HOMES

Rates then kept moving steadily up until 1982, when they took a big jump to 17 percent and beyond before they dipped again.

You can trace the sales volume of real estate simply by following interest rates. When the rates were low, volume was surging; when they got high it dropped to nothing.

## INFLATION AND REAL ESTATE

While interest rates determine the sales volume, inflation is the big force moving prices of real estate up. About 1975 inflation began taking off. In the late 1970s we had a situation where inflation was rapidly rising and people were looking for ways to protect themselves from the loss of value of the dollar. Residential real estate was one logical choice.

What's fascinating is that between 1974 and about 1979, when inflation was accelerating, mortgage rates remained low. This means that during rising inflation (and rising housing prices), low mortgage rates kept the volume of the market high. In other words, during that period it was ever so easy to buy a house that was rapidly rising in value.

Consider this: during that period of time the average mortgage rate was only 9 percent. But the average house appreciation was well over 15 percent! It doesn't take a genius to see why being a middleman and buying and selling houses paid off in the late 1970s. *The single biggest reason for the real estate boom we had was that we had a combination of low mortgage rates and high inflation.*

But if the boom was caused by high inflation and low interest rates, the decline in real estate which followed was caused by just the opposite conditions—high interest rates and low inflation. It is equally important to understand that when interest rates are high and inflation is low, people who previously fought to get into the market either won't or can't buy.

## THE NEW RULES

Times have indeed changed. We aren't likely to see another real estate boom comparable to the late 1970s again for quite some time. The reason is that lenders today have created conditions where low interest rates on mortgages and high inflation may be impossible. They have created mortgages which are inflation-sensitive.

Most mortgages issued today have adjustable interest rates. When inflation goes up one percentage point today, you can be assured that mortgage rates will go up as well. As long as money in general remains tight (remember the liquidity challenge we discussed earlier), low mortgage-interest rates will not reappear.

We can expect the following for the remainder of the decade:

> Inflation will rise *and* fall
>
> Interest rates will rise and fall *with inflation*
>
> We won't have high inflation with low mortgage-interest rates

"I've heard some people say that what really counts is not inflation or interest rates, but demand," said Dorothy. "These people point out that there is a great pent-up de-

## BUYING AND HOLDING
## BRAND NEW HOMES

mand for housing in this country. The children of the baby-boom generation are growing up, creating families, and looking for houses. This means there's a never-ending stream of home buyers. Why doesn't this shoot prices up?"

I explained that the baby-boom demand has been oversold by some promoters. Most baby-boomers are not wealthy. They are the ones most affected by higher prices and higher mortgage-interest rates. The truth is that while there are many, many baby-boomers who would love to buy their own home, ownership of homes in the U.S. by families actually *decreased* between 1980 and 1983 (by about 1 percent). That's the first decrease in more than a decade. The baby-boomers can't help the market if they can't afford to buy.

## HOW TO DEAL WITH
## THE NEW TIMES

"I see what you mean about times changing," said Dorothy. "I lost because I tried to be a middleman after the market had crested. I guess the only thing for me to do is forget real estate as an investment."

Yes and no, I quickly explained. I was merely saying that the days of quick resales are probably a thing of the past. Yes, the days of being a middleman through high-leveraged deals are over for a while. Nothing-down and almost-nothing-down purchases don't make much sense today.

Yes, if quick deals are all you want to do, then my suggestion is do get out of the market. If you can't quickly resell for a profit, being a middleman does you no good. Just as our farmer got destroyed by the high cost of storing his pork bellies once the boom market ended, when you buy for little or nothing down you get eaten up by the high costs of holding high-leveraged real estate.

No, don't get out if you want to make huge long-term profits. Real estate still offers ample opportunity here. Both women looked puzzled. Let's analyze exactly why you both lost, I said. Let's look at the technique that didn't work.

## NOTHING-DOWNERS OFTEN LOSE OVER THE LONG HAUL

We could say that the reason you've both lost is *because* you bought for little or nothing down in today's market. They looked at each other. "We thought we were doing the right thing. Are you saying that buying with little down is what worked against us?" Beverly asked.

Indeed it did, I pointed out. In real estate as in anything else, the piper must be paid. Little- or nothing down transactions almost always result in higher carrying costs. These costs may come in the form of higher payments each month or they may be deferred as higher costs coming later. But whether you pay these higher carrying costs immediately or later, either way you end up *paying more*.

Of course, if you can resell for a big profit in a short time, you don't care about those higher carrying costs. In a boom market when you plan to resell in six months or less, who cares if your payments are $1,500 a month and your rental income is only $750. You're going to sell right away for a big profit anyhow. But in a normal market such as exists today where you can plan only to hold over the long term, these heavy carrying costs can destroy any hopes of profit you may have.

"What you're saying," broke in Carrie, "is that we shouldn't be just looking at how cheaply we can get into a property. What we should be looking at is how much it's going to cost us to hold that property."

## TODAY'S PROFITS IN REAL ESTATE

As we've seen, yesterday the key to success was getting in for nothing, tying up as many houses as possible, and reselling for a big profit. Today the key to success in real estate can best be defined as *sustaining your ownership*. Today the key is to buy a property that can carry itself for at least ten years without being a drain on you. In other words, the income from rents should cover the principal, interest, taxes, and insurance over a very long time. Another way of saying this is that today you should be able to buy a piece of property and forget about it.

Both Carrie and Dorothy looked at each other with puzzled expressions. "You mean you want us to buy a house and then just put it on the shelf?"

That's right, I told them. Today the easiest way to get into the market is to be an *inactive* investor. That's not the same as a *passive* investor, however. A passive investor lets someone else invest for him or her. An inactive investor just invests in his or her spare time. An inactive investor makes real estate investments only occasionally.

## SPARE-TIME INVESTING

Our obvious objective in investing is to make money, but we need to match our energy to what our investment field can bear.

We've seen how residential real estate in the late 1970s to early 1980s allowed middlemen to make money. But being a middleman tends to be a full-time job. You're always out there scouting up new properties and finding buyers for ones that you already own. The more energy you expend, the faster you get rich. As long as the market is quickly moving up, the name of the game is action.

Today, however, rapid price acceleration and rapid turnover are no longer realistic. Rather, what we need to do is hang on for a long time. This changes our investment strategy enormously.

Today the market simply isn't hot enough for most of us to be full-time investors. Rather, what works best is being a part-time investor. This person keeps his or her regular job and uses spare time to make real estate investments over a ten-year period. (Of course, should a new boom occur in the meantime, our investor is always ready to jump in and take full-time advantage of the situation.)

Today what makes sense for most investors is *not* to quit their present jobs, is *not* to devote eighty hours a week to real estate, is *not* to think property to the exclusion of all else. What makes sense is to give real estate a few hours of quality time a month. Remember, today you're buying to hold long-term.

"There's something I don't understand," interrupted Carrie. "If I buy and then quickly resell for more, I've made a profit. But where's the profit if I just buy and hold? If you're inactive, how do you make your money?"

## THREE METHODS OF PROFITING BY HOLDING HOMES LONG-TERM

I pointed out that there were three methods of making money on property by owning and holding over the long term:

## BUYING AND HOLDING
## BRAND NEW HOMES

1. Tax advantages. Real estate still offers excellent tax advantages. These can reduce your current income (act like a tax shelter), and this is a source of annual profit that must not be overlooked.

2. Mortgage payoff. When you hold property over a long period of time, the tenants pay off the mortgage for you. The trick is to get a mortgage that is quickly reduced. (We'll see how shortly.)

3. Appreciation. Buying certain kinds of homes in specific areas can assure us that we will have good price appreciation over the long term. We can get our money out later (perhaps ten years later) by either refinancing or selling.

"It sounds awfully slow to me," said Dorothy. "You could wait ten years before you made any sizable chunk of money the way you're talking."

"Yes," agreed Carrie, "it's hardly making a quick buck."

## "GUARANTEED" WEALTH

I explained that what they said was in a way both true and not true. Certainly waiting ten years for your profit is a very long time. However, it can *almost* be guaranteed wealth. And that's worth waiting for.

Further, sometimes *quick* profits are really illusory. This is particularly the case in real estate where the profits may come in the form of "paper" (second or third mortgages on property) that may eventually turn out to be worthless or worth only a fraction of their face value.

I pointed out that over the last few years I had seen a phenomenon that I hadn't encountered before—quick and broke millionaires. These people made their million in a few years and then, in a much shorter time, lost it. I can't tell you how many people I've met who were wealthy in 1981 and broke by 1984. They "Ping-Ponged" their investment energy. They went up fast and they came down even faster.

The idea is not to say, "I want to make a million dollars in one year." Even if you succeed, that million may be so tied up that you'll lose it in a market turn the next year. The idea is to say, "I want to make a million dollars in real estate over the next ten years and keep it all!"

"But how do we do that?" Both Carrie and Dorothy were determined to get an answer.

There are several methods, but they all come back to the same idea. *You want to find a house which can sustain itself over a long period of time.* In other words, the income you can expect from rent will at least cover the expenses of mortgage principal, interest, taxes, and insurance.

"That doesn't seem possible in today's market," Carrie observed. "Prices of homes are so high that it's almost impossible finding one where you can break even."

I agreed it sometimes is hard, but it is far from impossible. Finding the "sustainable house" involves locating the right mixture of three essential ingredients:

1. Rental market
2. House price
3. Financing

### THE RENTAL MARKET

*You want to be in a strong rental market.* In most areas of the country the number of new homes being built is down

## BUYING AND HOLDING BRAND NEW HOMES

tremendously from a decade ago. At the same time the overall population, and particularly those forming new families, is up. People have to live somewhere. If they can't buy (because of high prices and high interest rates), they'll rent. While some areas of the country do not have a strong rental market because of industry layoffs or other factors, most areas do. You want to invest only in an area where there is a strong rental market. (If you're not sure of your area, just go out and pretend to be trying to rent a house. You can find out what the market is like in a few hours.)

*In strong rental markets, rents are high and getting higher.* In these markets the house that rented for $500 monthly a year ago is probably renting for $600 or more now. It's important to understand that this increase does not come about because of inflation. Rather it's because of demand. There are relatively few houses for rent and lots of people chasing them.

"But people can't afford higher rents," Carrie pointed out.

*People can afford higher rents today,* I said. People today are mingling. Instead of a single person renting an apartment, often three single people will pool their resources and rent a house together. Their combined incomes allow them to pay higher rents. This is the case not only for singles, but for divorced people and the elderly as well. By combining households, people are able to pay today's higher rents. (If mingling appeals to you, I suggest my book *Mingles, A Home Buying Guide for Unmarried Couples,* McGraw-Hill, 1984.)

*The right kind of house can always be rented for more money.* Since many people are mingling these days, often the best rental house is one which will accommodate several unrelated people. Many builders of new homes are recognizing this and are building "mingles houses." These have the equivalent of two or three master bedrooms. In other words, each bedroom has a separate bath. And the common areas are easily accessed.

In a rental this means finding a home which is easily partitioned into different living areas. Houses with several bathrooms adjacent to bedrooms are ideal.

"What you're saying is that it is possible to command a very high rent for the right house in the right area," Carrie said. I nodded. "But doesn't rent control keep rental income down?" she asked.

*Rent control doesn't usually affect single-family homes.* In most communities rent control is directed at apartment-house owners. Those who own only a single-family house usually aren't affected. In addition, many communities which enthusiastically adopted rent control only a few years ago are reconsidering it today. (Los Angeles is an example.) The city fathers have found that rent control (like oil and gas control or wage and price control or any other control) has harmful long-term effects. In real estate it acts to stifle future development that could act naturally to bring prices down. It also results in owners not keeping up the property they own.

All of which means that if you buy the right house in the right area, (1) there's going to be lots of tenants wanting to rent your house and (2) you're going to be able to charge a fairly high rent and be able to increase that rent as time goes by.

The result is that looking long-term, you can count on a fairly high rental income immediately and an increasing rental income as the years go by. This means that even if you can't quite break even on your monthly ex-

BUYING AND HOLDING
BRAND NEW HOMES

penses on a house today, chances are you'll be able to break even in a year or two. While I don't like buying a house today which shows a carrying-charge loss, I always figure that I can accept a small loss each month as long as I can expect that house to sustain itself at least within three years. In today's rental market, that's a realistic possibility.

## THE PRICE OF HOUSING

"Even if we get guaranteed tenants and high rents, the price of houses seems too high to buy these days," Dorothy lamented. "What with high mortgage-interest rates, the monthly payments end up so terrible that no one can afford them—either me or a tenant!"

Prices certainly are high, I noted. But the key to getting the monthly costs down is to keep the price down. High prices today are largely a holdover from the big price run-up of the late 1970s. Price appreciation in most areas has been fairly constant for several years now. If that continues we can expect the *relative* price of houses—that is, price in comparison to incomes and rents—to actually decline.

But what's important to understand is that there are still many lower-priced homes available. It is still possible to buy a house in a reasonably good area for $75,000 or less in most communities today. (The exceptions are the high-priced suburban areas such as part of southern California, the San Francisco Bay area, New York, Chicago, and similar places. People in those areas may have to travel outside of their immediate surrounding communities to get good sustainable real estate.)

An alternative to traveling great distances, however, I told Dorothy, was to buy a brand-new home. Today new homes in areas adjacent to heavily developed communities can be the best real estate investment buy.

Dorothy looked shocked. "Buy a brand-new home? I thought you had to live in it to get financing on a new home?"

Usually you do, I answered, which makes it even more of a bargain. We'll get right back to that, but first let's discuss the final consideration when buying an investment house—the financing.

## THE FINANCING

As we've pointed out, financing today is not the wonderful thing it was just a few years ago. Any financing today is bad compared to the past. Nevertheless, there are some kinds of financing that we can live with.

"But what about creative financing?" asked Dorothy. "Isn't that the way to get into property?"

Forget creative financing. As we noted earlier, the piper must be paid. Either you pay monthly or you pay after a few years or you pay when you sell. *But you still pay.* The only time that creative financing works to the real advantage of the buyer is when it works to the real disadvantage of the seller. In today's market, sellers have been warned about those investors who come by trying to tie up property with nothing down but promises. Today only desperate and ignorant sellers will agree to creative financing. You can go looking for those sellers, but often the reason they want to sell is because their house is a lemon or is terribly overpriced. Yes, they'll give you a great deal, if you'll take over their great headache.

*For the long term* the best thing you can do is to get the lowest-rate loan possible.

## BUYING AND HOLDING BRAND NEW HOMES

## THE BUY-A-NEW-HOME-
## TO-RENT METHOD

I suggested that we get down to nuts and bolts. We first discussed Dorothy's investment situation.

Dorothy and her husband, Todd, had been married two years. They had no children and were looking to get started making their financial fortune. They both had well-paying jobs and they had substantial savings. Real estate seemed a logical first step for them. However, they had gone out and purchased three properties for nothing down. They had lost thousands of dollars in carrying charges, and then they had lost the properties as well. They still, however, had nearly $5,000 in savings.

"I'm not too lucky, am I," said Dorothy.

I pointed out that luck didn't have anything to do with it. (Reread the second chapter if you don't know why.)

Things weren't as bad as they seemed. What Dorothy really needed was a plan, a method for steadily acquiring property and building her fortune. Because she was living in an apartment, I told her the plan for her was obvious. She should buy a house to live in, hold it for a while until she accumulated enough money, then rent out her house and buy another to live in. In this fashion she could move from house to house acquiring a great many houses over a ten-year period.

"What's the difference between that and what I did before?" Dorothy asked.

I pointed out that the difference was enormous. Before she bought strictly with an eye to quickly reselling. Now she would be buying to live in and to rent for a long period. Because she was buying to live in and rent out, she would choose different kinds of property than she had before. She would be very concerned now that the property could "sustain" itself.

You're not going to be a middleman anymore. You're going to be providing rental space for tenants. You're going to become a landlord.

The key to making it work, I explained, was to put your desires in perspective. I then asked her a question, "Would you be willing to live modestly for several years if you were virtually guaranteed that after that time you could live in a wealthy fashion?"

"It depends on how long I'd have to live modestly," replied Dorothy.

I explained that I was speaking of as long as ten or so years. That's how long it might take in real estate in today's market. (Of course, that time frame could be reduced enormously by investing in some of the other areas discussed in other parts of this book.)

"I suppose it would be OK," Dorothy replied, "if there was a sure payoff at the end."

The payoff is virtually guaranteed, I explained, because you can see it coming as you go. If you ever get off-track, you know it immediately and can change course.

Because both you and your husband have a good income and have some money to invest, the idea is to buy a house you can afford to purchase today. You can make the monthly payments on the house out of your regular income. You move into that house, live in it for a year or so, and then, when you've accumulated a bit more money, rent it out. (That's where getting a modest house pays off. You're sure that the house you buy can be rented for the monthly payments.) Now you buy another.

"Where do I get the money for the down payment for the next house?" Dorothy asked.

## BUYING AND HOLDING BRAND NEW HOMES

You can save, but more important you can let Uncle Sam provide some of it, I explained. Remember you can deduct the interest and taxes you pay on your home from your federal and state incomes taxes. If your taxes and interest come to $750 a month, over twelve months that's $9,000. Assuming you're in a 40 percent tax bracket (federal and state combined), that comes to about $3,600 in savings in just a year.

"Will that be enough?" Carrie was surprised.

I explained that it could go a long way, particularly if you bought the right way so you ended up with only a single, large, affordable loan.

### LEARNING FROM THE OLD DAYS

I pointed out that in the "old days" the standard method of getting started in real estate was to buy a home of your own, live in it for a while, then rent it out while you bought another home. That was how I and many others got started. Look at it this way, I said. Suppose you have a fifteen-year mortgage on your house (we'll see how to get such financing at the end of this chapter). If the mortgage was $100,000, at the end of ten years that house will be more than half paid off.

Just by cutting the mortgage in half, you've suddenly made yourself $50,000. In addition, if the house appreciated $50,000 in value over ten years (that works out to only about 3 percent a year) you've now made yourself a second $50,000. And if you've rented it out to tenants, they have made most of the mortgage payments for you during that time!

Further, if you bought one such house every year for ten years, think of how much solid wealth you would have acquired in your equity. That's not paper profits—that's solid real estate equity.

True, you won't retire next year by this method. But it is almost guaranteed that in ten years you will be able to retire.

### GETTING THE PROFITS OUT

"It sounds great," said Dorothy, "But can I get the profits out after ten years?"

Yes, easily. There are two ways I pointed out. You can sell the house, but this really defeats the purpose of stabilizing your wealth. Or you can refinance. By refinancing *after ten years and not before*, you get your money out and you still own the property. Ten years later you can refinance again.

I explained that my father, who was also a real estate broker, used to speak of this technique as a "money tree." He would say, "It's like growing your own profits. Once the tree is planted, you just nurture it and keep it going and it will provide for you thereafter."

"It sounds fantastic," said Dorothy. "How do I get started?"

### BUYING NEW HOMES

I told Dorothy that what she and Todd might seriously consider doing is buying a brand-new house. For the first time in nearly a decade there are distinct investment advantages in buying brand-new homes from developers.

Dorothy looked surprised. "I've never heard anyone advise buying a new home for investment," she said. "I've always been told to look for resales."

## BUYING AND HOLDING BRAND NEW HOMES

Times change, I reminded her. I pointed out that prior to about 1974 new homes were the best investment buys you could make. The reason was that they cost considerably less on the average than older homes. However, that all changed in the second half of the 1970s.

The median cost of new homes first exceeded that of old ones in about 1974. Prior to then, standard advice for investors was to buy a new home, put in a yard, wait a while for prices to appreciate, and then look to sell.

After 1974, however, due to inflation of land prices and building costs, the resale market was so much cheaper than the new home market that everyone jumped there. Buying a resale suddenly made sense because that's where the profits were. But we've come full circle. Today the new home once again is often the better buy for the beginning investor.

"You mean new homes are once again cheaper than resales?"

Almost, I pointed out, the gap is narrowing dramatically.

Today the new home once again makes investment sense. But what really makes new homes a great opportunity for the *long-term* investor is the chance to participate in the growth of a residential area from infancy to maturity (and gain the profits along the way).

"What do you mean by 'growth'?" asked Carrie. "Do neighborhoods grow?"

## APPRECIATION IN PRICE
## THROUGH NEIGHBORHOOD GROWTH

Yes, they do grow, I pointed out. "What you're saying," broke in Dorothy, "is that by buying a new home, just the growth of the neighborhood will be enough to give good price appreciation."

I nodded, adding that you also had to buy in a desirable area. During the late 1970s, early 1980s, inflation was so high and financing so easy that buying a resale and then just sitting on it for six months made great sense. Today with inflation frequently lower and with interest rates tied to inflation, that makes little sense. The appreciation of resales is too small. It's far better to get the advantage of neighborhood growth.

Think of it like this, I suggested. Almost everything can be spoken of as having a life span and as going through various stages of life. People, for example go through infancy, adolescence, middle age, and old age before death.

Homes behave in a similar fashion. Neighborhoods go through the similar stages in their economic life. Assuming we have a desirable area, there's an infancy stage right after the house is first built when the owners are putting in yards, fixing up the house, and getting "off the ground." Then there's the adolescence when the lawns are all in, the fencing all up, and the neighborhood suddenly blossoms as a cohesive whole instead of being just a jumble of raw land and new houses. The area now is usually more desirable and prices take a skip up. Finally there's maturity when the trees and landscaping have reached full growth and the houses are considered to be in a well developed and mature neighborhood. Prices due to neighborhood development are at a maxium now. They will continue to rise now only if general inflation pushes them higher. This long middle stage can last for decades.

Finally there is a period when the house becomes obsolete and less desirable. Dilapidation occurs, lawns and landscaping deteriorate, and prices decline (often seen as a failure to advance in spite of inflation). This old age of the house eventually ends when, perhaps thirty to eighty years after it's built, the house is torn down to make way for commercial or other residential development. (In an initially undesirable neighborhood the area could end up blighted and potentially worthless.)

## THE BEST TIME TO BUY

"I've always heard the best time to buy was when the house was in a mature neighborhood," said Dorothy, "You got the best financing and the best opportunity for appreciation."

I pointed out that as we had seen, this was certainly true in the late 1970s. However, today financing is tough all around. Assumable loans are difficult to get. Sellers are wary of creative financing techniques. And many mature neighborhoods aren't seeing much appreciation.

Today things are different. Today the time to buy is when the house is brand-new. Chances are you'll get better financing. But more important, you'll be able to take advantage of the price skip when the neighborhood goes from infancy to maturity. Buying new in a desirable area today, you stand an excellent chance of getting enormous appreciation over a ten-year period.

## BETTER FINANCING

In addition, unlike the situation a few years back, today the better financing is available in new homes.

"You mean builders can get better loans?" Carrie asked.

Yes and no, I replied. Sometimes because he is borrowing for a whole tract a builder can indeed negotiate a slightly better interest rate. However, that rate is usually only a quarter of a percent or so better than you could otherwise get.

The real advantage of new-home financing comes from two facts: First, the builders are determined to sell their houses, so they may have already shopped around for the best mortgages available. (This is not always the case. Some builders get tied into the lender who gave them the construction loan and are forced to offer lesser-quality financing.)

## BUY DOWNS

Second, builders will frequently buy down the financing to a point where it becomes attractive to buyers.

"Buy down? What's that," asked Dorothy.

Essentially it just means that the builder pays the difference between the going interest rate and a lower interest rate so that the buyer can get a better deal. For example, the current market rate might be 13 percent. To get sales, however, the builder might offer the loan to the buyer at 12 percent, absorbing the 1 percent difference himself.

This is done through the payment of a one-time fee called points. Typically a builder can buy down a loan for 1 point per each quarter percent of rate reduction. Therefore, to get a $100,000 loan reduced from 13 percent to 12 percent might cost the builder $4,000 (1 percent, or $1,000, for each ¼ or in some cases ⅛ percent reduction).

"You mean when I buy a house with a $100,000 mortgage and I get a loan rate of 12 percent when the market mortgage rate is 13 percent, it's cost the builder an extra $4,000?" Carrie couldn't believe it.

## BUYING AND HOLDING BRAND NEW HOMES

I explained that the buy-down cost was a rule of thumb. In some cases it might be 1 point per ⅛ percent. The amount varied depending on how much mortgage money was available for lending.

"You're not getting anything for free," Dorothy interrupted. "You can be darn sure the builder is adding that $4,000 to the cost of the home. Sure you're getting a lower interest rate, but you're paying for it with a higher price!"

Carrie looked at me to see if Dorothy was correct. I nodded that she was. Carrie then asked, "If that's the case, what's the advantage?"

The big advantage is that you get a lower than market-rate loan. If you were planning to quickly resell, then of course the thousands extra you are paying in price wouldn't be worth it. But if you're going to hold for ten years or longer, then that extra few thousand is quickly forgotten and the lower interest rate and lower monthly payments over the long haul become more valuable to you.

"What about an adjustable- or a fixed-rate mortgage?"

I replied that it was very hard to decide between them today, but that we'd look into each later.

"But why haven't other people told me to buy a new home?" asked Dorothy. "Surely what you're saying should be known by most people in real estate."

## THE BEST-KEPT SECRET
## IN REAL ESTATE

The reason most advisers don't tell you about buying *new* homes is that you go to them seeking *investment* property. Almost by definition new homes are not investment property.

Carrie and Dorothy looked puzzled.

It's quite simple, I explained. In order to get loans on new homes the builder *almost always* has to be certain that the buyers will *actually live* in the property. In fact, moving and occupying the house yourself is often a loan requirement. Since most investors don't plan on occupying the property they buy, advisers don't mention new homes.

"So I'll have to move in."

Yes, I replied. But you have to live somewhere, and you want to move out of your present apartment anyhow, don't you? So why not buy a house and move in?

## THE DOWN PAYMENT

"What about the down payment," asked Dorothy. "We have only $5,000."

To many people $5,000 would seem like a fortune. However, depending on the price of the house, that should be adequate. I pointed out that there were two ways to buy new homes that involved low down payments (not to be confused with "nothing down," which often implies undesirable creative financing).

The first method was a PMI loan. This was simply a conventional loan which the lender had insured with a private insurance company. Normally on a conventional loan, the maximum loan to value ratio (how big a loan in relationship to the value of the property) is 80 percent. When the loan is insured, however, that jumps to 90 or even 95 percent.

I pointed out that if they bought a $60,000 house under a PMI loan, they would need only 10 percent, or $6,000 down. Of course, there would also be closing costs.

"Not bad," commented Dorothy, "but not terrific. I'd

still be short. Besides, finding a new $60,000 home in my area could be tough."

## THE NEW ADVANTAGES OF GOVERNMENT-INSURED LOANS

I suggested an FHA loan as an alternative. These were extremely popular in the 1950s and 1960s. They lost favor in the 1970s but are once again becoming very popular.

I pointed out that with a property value of $90,000 the maximum FHA loan was $86,000 (as of this writing). That's only $4,000 down, leaving some money for closing costs (which might be negotiated lower than normal with the builder). At 12 percent interest, with taxes and insurance, that comes to about $950 a month. In addition the FHA is now insuring PAMs (partially amortized mortgages) with fifteen-year balloons (you can renegotiate these), which give significantly lower payments.

Dorothy seemed shocked. "You mean I can get into a $90,000 house for only $4,000 down without any creative financing at all?"

I nodded.

"Now let me get this straight," she continued. "I live there for a year or so. By then I've saved up another $5,000 (partly from the tax advantages of home ownership). I move out of this house, rent it, and buy another. How do I know I can rent the house for $950 a month?"

## CHECKING OUT RENTALS BEFORE YOU BUY

Nine hundred fifty dollars a month may seem like a high rental. But as we've already seen, if you're in the right market with the right kind of a house it can be done. If you rent to two or three singles (mingles) or a family where both spouses work, it's not an excessive rent at all. This is particularly true if the location is pleasant to live in and near work sites for the tenants. Remember, I pointed out, you're not renting out a twenty-year-old house as you were when you invested under the old rules. You're renting out a virtually brand-new house in a brand-new neighborhood. Many people are willing to pay extra to get that.

"It sounds almost too good to be true," exclaimed Dorothy. "Let's get started!"

Just remember, I told her, the reason this works for you is that:

1. You're willing to live in the house. (FHA loans require that you move in.)
2. You have the down payment.
3. You're making enough outside income to make the monthly payments.
4. You select an area and house where high rental incomes are possible.

However, there are many people and houses which don't fit this category.

### LOCATION FIRST, MIDDLE, AND LAST!

We put aside talk and went out into the field looking at new housing tracts. We tried to keep to those whose prices were under $100,000 so our mortgage payments would re-

## BUYING AND HOLDING BRAND NEW HOMES

main relatively low. Once we had identified the appropriate tracts, we checked each out for location.

In real estate, location is everything. If you're well located, then you can be assured your property will be desirable to others. If it's desirable, it will make a big skip in price between infancy and adulthood. Finally, in such an area you won't have trouble finding tenants who are willing to pay a higher rent.

On the other hand, if you're poorly located, then no matter what you do, you'll find that the house never appreciates much in value. And finding tenants can be a real problem.

After we had spent a day searching out new housing, Dorothy moaned, "All the good locations seem to be too expensive."

Naturally, I pointed out, builders are going to charge more for better areas. The solution is to either go further out (but not too far, as that will adversely affect the rental market) or *buy a smaller home.*

"I thought bigger was better," said Dorothy.

Not necessarily. Today smallness is valued. A two-bedroom home where each bedroom can be used as a master bedroom by two unmarried people sharing the house can be a real winner in the rental market. (I pointed out that Dorothy had to check the deed and with local government authorities to be sure there were no restrictions on having unmarried couples rent if she was planning to have mingles tenants.)

The next day she found an ideal house in a well-located tract. Most of the homes in the tract sold in the $120,000 to $130,000 range, but there was one two-bedroom model for $95,000. Since Dorothy and Todd had no children, she felt it was ideal for her. She put down a deposit and was on her way to making her real estate fortune.

## THE FIXER-UPPER MARKET

Carrie seemed depressed after that. Dorothy was already started, but Carrie still had the two houses she had bought for $10,000 down apiece. They were draining her. Besides, she had almost no cash left and her income wasn't enough to qualify for either an FHA or PMI mortgage. "I guess I'm out of luck," she moaned.

Not at all, I said, trying to be cheerful. You can get back into winning real estate by playing the fixer-upper market. Carrie was not afraid of hard work and she was willing to spend her spare time renovating an old house. I pointed out she was the ideal person for the old tried and true method of getting ahead for those with little cash—fixer-uppers. And you can do it in your spare time.

"But what about those two dogs I have." (She was referring to her investment houses.)

I pointed out that they would be her ticket to the fixer-upper. She could simply trade them to the seller for the down payment.

"Why would any seller want to own my houses? I lose money on them every month."

"Never assume you know what a seller's motives are." I pointed out that some sellers were in high income-tax brackets. They were looking for "losers," houses where the income was far lower than the expenses. They would rent them out, depreciate them, and take the overall loss as a tax shelter. There were undoubtedly many, many sellers out there who would look at her "dogs" as godsends. But first we had to identify the right area.

## THE RIGHT AREA
## FOR A FIXER-UPPER

When you buy a fixer-upper, I explained, you cross the boundaries between middleman and producer. You're producing and your product is the fixing up of the house. But you're also a middleman because you're vitally concerned about the margin, the difference between your buying price and your selling price.

I explained that there had to be enough margin to pay for all the costs of fixing up plus leave a profit. In today's market that usually meant finding one of two kinds of houses—either a run-down or a battered house in an expensive neighborhood. The condition of the house would keep the selling price low. The neighborhood would allow you to sell it (after the fix-up) for a profit.

"I can't believe neighborhood is that important," said Carrie. "I look at a house, not its neighbors."

I told Carrie I was willing to bet she was wrong. I told her she would probably not even look at a house for sale until she had already decided it was in a good neighborhood.

Consider this example I told her. Some twenty years ago after the San Fernando Valley had been developed (a suburban area of over a million people near Los Angeles), there were tracts that were in the center and others that were north and yet others south. At the time the price difference between houses in different tracts was negligible.

Yet over the years the houses on the south side of the Valley (south of Ventura Boulevard) in general far outstripped the other areas in terms of appreciation, often by a factor of two or three times. Those in the northern hills in general far outstripped the tracts in the center.

I asked Carrie where the best possible location would be to look for a fixer-upper. The lower-priced middle of the valley, the higher-priced north end, or the highest-priced south side?

Carrie thought a moment and said, "Probably the center. It has the lowest price, and I probably can afford to go there."

I suggested that she was wrong. If she was looking for the *largest margin* between her purchase and resale prices she was likely to find it in the more expensive areas. The difference between the buying price and selling price of a fixer-upper in a lower-priced area is usually too small to make the work worthwhile. There just isn't enough margin.

"But I won't be able to afford the higher-priced areas!" she exclaimed.

## BUYING LIKE A MIDDLEMAN

Now it's time to play the middleman, I suggested. You can use your two homes as the down payment. Then you can negotiate with a seller so that you get no monthly payments until after you've owned the property for one year. It's possible if the seller carries the financing. Then you'll either start making big payments or pay him off entirely.

That one year is your time frame. Once you've identified the house, you'll have one year to fix it up and sell it. Otherwise you'll probably lose it.

"I don't understand how to do that," stammered Carrie.

It's not that difficult. For example, you have the seller carry the mortgage. You agree to the interest rate the seller wants and the price (assuming it reflects the value of the

## BUYING AND HOLDING BRAND NEW HOMES

property). You insist, however, that there are no payments for a year. Some sellers will go along with you; others won't. The trick is to find one who will.

"In other words, I give the seller his price and interest rate; the seller gives me terms."

Precisely, I replied.

"But isn't that the creative financing you were warning us about earlier?"

It is a form of creative financing. However, my warning earlier had to do with properties that were already fixed up. Here we're concerned with distressed property, a house which for one reason or another has some detraction. A seller here will be more inclined to give favorable terms, and you'll know what the house's problem is. Now here's what we're looking for in terms of a house:

### WHAT TO LOOK FOR IN A FIXER-UPPER

**1.** *Location.* We've already said it should be in a choice location, one where there's ample margin to pay for your fixing up and for your profit.

**2.** A *run-down house.* Quite frankly these aren't as easy to come by as they used to be. Many investors worked the fixer-upper market dry during the late 1970s. But with the decline in real estate over the past couple of years, many more of them have come on the market and new ones appear all the time. It takes careful looking.

**3.** A *tiny house.* The idea here is to add on. Perhaps add a bedroom, bath, and dining room. Make a small house into a larger one and you can sometimes double the value—if the neighborhood is right.

**4.** *Convert.* Find a big house and make it into a duplex (where zoning allows). Take a run-down large house and make it into a place suitable for mingles. The opportunities here are limited only by your imagination (and zoning restrictions).

## GETTING STARTED

Off and on for nearly a month Carrie searched for the right house. She found many, but all seemed wrong for her. It wasn't until she found a medium-size home on a hill with a landslide on one side that she was convinced it was for her.

The surrounding homes sold in the $300,000 range. But because the landslide had knocked into one side of the house and the city had condemned the place, the seller was willing to let it go for $200,000.

We discussed the house. Carrie pointed out that the landslide had essentially done only superficial damage to the home. The city would allow the place to be inhabited once the damage had been corrected. The problem was the city required that the ground behind the hill be stabilized. The seller told her he had received a bid of $75,000 to put in a concrete retaining wall. That and the risk was why he was asking a lower price and was willing to accede to her terms.

Carrie put up her two houses and gave the seller a mortgage for $180,000 all due and payable with interest in one year, no payments before then.

Then she got started. Using ingenuity she used telephone poles driven into the bank with heavy retaining planks to prevent future slides. A tractor cleaned out the old slide

## BUYING AND HOLDING BRAND NEW HOMES

in two days. Then workmen quickly rebuilt the damaged side of the house.

"The seller thought the only way to stabilize the land was with a huge concrete retaining wall. I got my old telephone poles drilled in place for less than $15,000. The total cost of fixing up the place came to only $20,000, which I borrowed on the property!"

Within two months Carrie was ready to offer the house for sale. She put it on the market at $325,000 "by owner" and sold for $300,000. (Remember, it was a highly desirable area.) When the escrow closed, after all expenses she had a check in her pocket for over $70,000.

"I'm off to my next house!" she said. I smiled and pointed out that even with taxes, she had made a bundle.

### FINANCING RESIDENTIAL REAL ESTATE

After their successful first deals, Dorothy, Carrie, and I got together to discuss some of the problems and concerns inherent in investing in real estate today. The first had to do with financing.

#### Adjustable Versus Fixed-Rate Mortgages

"I've heard that the adjustable-interest-rate mortgages (ARMs) were a good deal for a buyer. You can get in for much less than in the old fixed rate." Carrie offered.

I pointed out they might get a buyer in, but usually they meant rapidly increasing payments over the first five years of the mortgage. In most cases they simply deceived buyers into thinking they were getting a better deal than they really were.

WEALTH
BUILDERS

Besides, what we need to do is to think of what would be the best mortgage for an investor who needs to hold the property for a long term, not for someone who wants to buy and quickly resell.

The best mortgage almost always is a fixed-rate loan. The reason simply is that the fixed rate reflects the true mortgage market at the time you get it. The adjustable, on the other hand, covers up the real rate. Let's take a quick example:

You obtain an adjustable-rate mortgage where the beginning rate is 10 percent at a time when the market (fixed) rate is 12½ percent. Are you getting a bargain?

Probably not. In such a loan typically the rate is allowed to rise 1 to 2 percent a year up to a maximum of perhaps 5 percent based on an index. Let's say that at the time you are applying for the loan the index is the Federal Reserve's cost-of-funds rate and that it is at 10 percent.

Usually adjustable loans are written at 2½ percent *above* the cost-of-funds index. (That makes sense—that 2½ percent is the lender's profit between the cost of borrowing and the return from lending.) This means that the *"true rate"* of the adjustable mortgage is 10 percent (cost-of-funds index) *plus* 2½ percent or 12½ percent. In other words although your adjustable may have a 10 percent rate *the first year*, if the index were to remain the same and not move at all, your loan would quickly rise within a year or two to 12½ percent.

What's important to see here is that interest rates don't have to go up for your loan to go up in cost. Your loan started out artificially lower and has to rise to get to its proper level.

"What you're saying is that there's no free meal in mortgages," Carrie commented.

## BUYING AND HOLDING
## BRAND NEW HOMES

That's exactly right. At least with a fixed-rate loan you know where you stand. And if interest rates should drop in the future, you can always refinance to a new lower fixed-rate loan.

### Fifteen-Year Financing

"You once said that it was possible to get fifteen-year loans. How do I do that?" asked Dorothy.

I explained that it was easy. The thing to remember about loan terms is that you pay the maximum interest in the first years of a loan. For example, I pointed out that a $50,000 loan at 12 percent interest for thirty years had a monthly payment of $514.31. Then I asked her how much of that $514 she thought went to principal and how much to interest?

Dorothy thought a while and then said, "I doubt that more than $100 goes to principal, with the rest to interest."

I nodded and pointed out that during the first year, out of the $514.31 payment only about $14 went to paying off the loan; all the rest was interest! Dorothy looked surprised. I added that before that $50,000 mortgage was paid off, the borrower would have made total interest payments (exclusive of principal) of $135,152!

Dorothy was incredulous. "I never realized so much of the loan went to interest."

It's largely a function of the term, I explained. There's so much interest mainly because the loan is dragged out over thirty years. Now, let's consider that same $50,000 loan at 12 percent interest; only this time let's figure a fifteen-year term. The total interest paid this way is $58,002. By paying off the loan in half the time, you save $77,132 in interest charges:

## WEALTH BUILDERS

$50,000 mortgage at 12%
Total interest paid over 30 years   $135,152
Total interest paid over 15 years    58,002
             Savings   $77,152

"You save more than half the interest by paying it off at a faster rate," exclaimed Dorothy. "But of course you're paying twice as much each month."

That's the unusual thing, I pointed out. The difference in monthly payments between a thirty-year loan and a fifteen-year loan is not that great.

Monthly payment on a
$50,000 loan at 12% interest
     For 15 years   $600.11
     For 30 years    514.31
     Difference     $85.80

The reason for such a small difference in monthly payments is that most of the interest occurs in the first ten years of the loan. By taking out the loan for only fifteen years, the borrower essentially eliminates fifteen years of interest payments. That means that much more each month goes to principal, allowing for only a slight increase in monthly payments.

"So what you're saying is that I should get a fifteen-year instead of a thirty-year loan."

Not at all, I explained. Most lenders won't give fifteen-year loans; they want the big interest. Also, you want your payments as low as possible in the event there is an emergency. If you can't find a tenant for a month you want to be able to pay out as little as possible.

## BUYING AND HOLDING BRAND NEW HOMES

What I suggest doing is to get a thirty-year loan which includes a clause that *allows prepayment without penalty at any time.* Then each month simply add an additional amount to the mortgage payment to go to pay the principal. In the case of the mortgage described here, adding $85.80 per month to the payment would mean the loan would be repaid in fifteen years instead of thirty.

"Won't the mortgage company object?" asked Dorothy.

Certainly they will, I replied. They want you to pay interest, not principal. Also they don't like the extra bookkeeping. However, there's nothing they can do if your mortgage allows for prepayment without penalty at any time. And most modern mortgages have such a clause in them.

### TAX PROBLEMS COMING?

"Are there any drawbacks to owning real estate?" Dorothy finally asked.

I pointed out that managing rentals was always a headache, but most people learned fairly quickly. (There are also a number of excellent books on the market showing how to handle rentals.) What may become a real problem, however, are tax changes affecting real estate.

There are two kinds of changes afoot, one affecting depreciation, the other interest rates.

### DEPRECIATION

As of this writing, owners of *investment* property can depreciate it over a fifteen-year period. Legislation currently pending would increase that term probably to twenty years. For most owners of rental houses, this would be only a minor loss. The difference is actually only a few hundred dollars a year, depending, of course, on the depreciable value of the house.

## DISALLOWING INTEREST-RATE DEDUCTIONS

Of much greater concern, however, are proposals to disallow the deduction for interest paid on mortgages on some types of real estate. Dorothy shook her head. "I don't understand what you mean by 'disallowing interest deductions.' "

Currently, I explained, if you own a house you can always deduct the interest you pay on your mortgage from your federal income taxes. Over the last decade, however, many bills have been introduced in Congress which would reduce or eliminate this deduction.

It's unlikely that *all* interest deductions would be disallowed. However, the government is seeking ways to increase tax revenues to cover the enormous national debt. Some likely forms of this would be new legislation to *limit* the interest deductions allowed on a residence or on a second home.

If such legislation passes and becomes law, it could devastate the real estate market. Even if investment property were excluded, *any* elimination of the interest deduction would be a blow to real estate and would surely have an adverse affect on the market price of residential property.

"Are you saying I shouldn't invest because of this?" asked Dorothy.

I'm only saying the situation bears close watching.

## WRITING IT OUT

At the final meeting I had with Dorothy and Carrie, I asked how they were coming with their investments. Both replied they were doing well.

I then asked if they had each written out their investment plan. Dorothy took out a stack of paper. She had worked it out every month for the next ten years! I said that was admirable, but not to let the paperwork keep her from being flexible. Things might not always work out as she expected.

Carrie took out a small piece of paper. "It's my formula," she said. "It describes the house and location I'm looking for. It gives me a percentage for my margin. It tells me how much I must pay and how much I must sell a fixer-upper for. I look at it every time before I buy."

I said they both appeared to have done well. Carrie concluded, "It's not hard in real estate today. It's just different."

## TIMED BULLION RISKS

### RISK
Significant, depending on market turns

### WHEN TO BUY
Inflation—low
Interest rates—high

### WHEN TO SELL
Inflation—high
Interest rates—low to medium

### HOLDING PERIOD
Short to medium—1 to 6 months

### MINIMUM CASH REQUIRED
$100

### PROFIT POTENTIAL
Doubling (or more) of money

### SKILL REQUIRED
Substantial knowledge of field necessary

### EFFORT REQUIRED
Little

### MAJOR DIFFICULTY
Storage (money tied up without interest being paid to you)

### PROBLEMS
Delegalization possible, "rip-off artists" in field

# CHAPTER FIVE

# TIMED BULLION RISKS

George Golden and I met for lunch one afternoon, and he detailed the problems he had with gold. "I bought from a guy who I trusted implicitly," he said. "He assured me that gold was certain to go up in price. He said it had been down for so long, the only way it could go was up!

"I told him I didn't like the idea of keeping gold around the house or transporting it back and forth to a bank safe deposit box. He assured me there was nothing to be concerned about. His organization had created a secure depository in an isolated mountain range. I remember his words, 'It would take a hydrogen bomb to break into our vault!' I trusted him and invested $5,000. A few months later there was a big scandal. He commited suicide. The vault was nearly empty, and I lost all my money.

"Don't get me wrong, I still believe gold can be a good investment. I just want to know how to invest so that I can make a profit instead of getting taken again."

George was a member of the Future Millionaires' Investment Club. He and I were discussing how he could turn his fortunes around in bullion.

## BULLION MARKETS

I pointed out that gold as well as silver and the other two more commonly purchased precious metals, platinum and palladium, each had its ups and downs. Many people had literally made fortunes in them by outguessing the market. But there were tricks to investing in the field. The first key to George's success was to get a better handle on what made precious metals go up or down in price. The second key was for George to come up with a secure purchase plan that made sense.

## WHAT IS BULLION?

To begin I pointed out that a common misconception was that there was a *bullion market*. That simply wasn't the way it worked. Rather there were separate markets for each of the precious metals. There was a market for gold, another for silver, yet another for platinum, and so on. Each market tended to respond to different influences. What they had in common was that when one market was sharply up or down it tended to pull the others along. If gold prices were up, then silver and the other metals would probably be up also.

That meant that in order to get a winning understanding of the field it was first necessary to understand how the individual markets worked and then how they related to each other.

## GOLD

The lure of gold is universal. Gold is treasured in every country in the world, even the Communist world. In fact, Russia is the globe's second largest gold producer. The Russians mine gold, refine it, and then sell it on the open market for dollars with which to buy grain and other vitally

## TIMED BULLION RISKS

needed products. This, in fact, suggests gold's major use—as a currency.

During World War II in occupied France, many French families survived after the French paper currency became worthless simply because they had gold. They could use it to buy food, shelter, and, on occasion, protection from the enemy. Today many French families still have gold coins hidden in the doorposts of their homes as a protection against a future catastrophe.

The same holds true in Indochina, in Korea, and in the Middle East. Many oil-rich countries and their sheiks hold a significant portion of their wealth in gold. The Shah of Iran's fortune, for example, was in large part formed of gold.

## THE CURRENCY OF LAST RESORT

In other words, gold is a currency of last resort. When paper money fails, gold retains its purchasing power. This has been true for countless centuries going all the way back to the times of the ancient Egyptians.

This role of gold as a last-resort currency helps to explain *one* element of its market. When a world crisis occurs and governments and individuals fear for their survival, many turn to gold. This sudden demand drives the metal's price up. This is the reason that every time there is a major world crisis we tend to read that the price of gold has jumped. Those who are worried about their survival (and others who are speculating) have driven the price up.

"What you're saying," interrupted George, "is that to

win at gold, I have to invest just before or just at the beginning of a world crisis."

That's a good start, I suggested; however, I pointed out, there are other *major* factors influencing the price of gold. Together with the one just discussed, they are:

1. World crisis
2. Inflation
3. Oil prices
4. Jewelry demand
5. Abundance of supply

## INFLATION

Gold by its very nature is scarce. There isn't a whole lot of it around. That's obviously the reason it's so expensive. However, its relative scarcity, when combined with its liquidity (remember it's recognized as a form of currency in every country in the world), makes it an excellent short-term hedge against inflation.

George looked puzzled. "I've heard that before, but I don't understand how it works."

It's simple to understand. Let's say an ounce of gold is worth $400. Now, let's further say that due to inflation, our currency declines in value dramatically (that means that we have far more dollars in circulation chasing either the same or fewer goods and services). What used to cost $1.00 now costs $1.25. We have a 25 percent inflation rate. What's happened to the price of gold?

To get the inflation we've, in effect, printed more dollars, but we still have the same amount of gold. Hence the value of gold *in terms of dollars* has gone up. It's gone

**TIMED BULLION RISKS**

up by 25 percent. An ounce of gold is now probably worth $500.

Notice that the intrinsic value of gold did not increase. Rather it's value relative to the dollar remained constant. When the dollar is worth less, gold (expressed in dollars) becomes worth more. That's the reason gold is an inflation hedge. It moves in the opposite direction. As inflation makes the dollar worth less, it also makes gold worth more.

Of course there's also anticipation. In times of inflation, speculators and investors want to quickly move into gold to take advantage of its hedging ability. They force the price up even higher than just inflation would warrant.

"That's simple enough to understand," said George. "I just watch for inflation, then buy gold."

## GOLD AND INTEREST RATES

It's still not quite that simple, I explained. Gold as an inflation hedge only works in the short term. It doesn't usually work with slow, gradual inflation over a long period of time.

George looked puzzled so I continued. If you have a thousand dollars to invest, you always have *two options*. You can stick your money in a speculative investment, such as gold. Or you can stick your money in a relatively risk-free area such as T-bills or money market accounts. Let's say inflation is running at 10 percent a year, where are you most likely to stick your money, in gold or T-bills?

George thought a moment, then said, "If inflation is that high, gold must be good. I'd buy gold."

"Okay," I said, "now let's change the conditions.

What if rates on virtually risk-free T-bills were paying 16 percent when inflation was at 10 percent? Would you rather take a risk on gold (which pays no interest while you hold it; which in fact usually costs something in storage and insurance charges), or would you choose the virtually risk-free 16 percent interest rate?"

George smiled. "You got me on that one," he said. "I'd have to take the risk-free interest rate. No risk, no bother, no worry. Why play around with gold?"

## GOLD, INFLATION, INTEREST RATES, AND CRISIS

You might have made the right move, I commented. But you still don't have enough information to be sure. Again George looked puzzled. What if, I speculated, at the same time as interest rates were 16 percent and inflation was 10 percent, a major war broke out in Europe, the Middle East, or even South America. Now, suddenly thousands, hundreds of thousands of people would feel threatened. They would decide that it was a good idea to get some gold "just in case." Suddenly the demand for gold as a currency of last resort would jump. What do you think would happen?

"The price of gold would probably go through the roof," agreed George.

That's similar to what happened in 1979, I noted. Inflation was rising rapidly (although interest rates remained fairly low), and Iran was holding Americans hostage, threatening to cause a major Middle East war.

George nodded. "I think I've got it. It's not just one thing I have to look out for, it's three. It's crisis, inflation, and interest rates, right?"

There are a few other things I pointed out.

## GOLD AND THE OIL CONNECTION

There is one commodity that the U.S., Western Europe, Japan, the entire Western world depends on for survival let alone prosperity—oil. Oil has become the lifeblood of our civilization. As the oil embargo of 1974 amply demonstrated, cut off our oil supplies and we change from a lion into a kitten.

Besides politics, however, oil also has an economic aspect. Everything we produce is either directly or indirectly related to oil. It's integral to the manufacture of fertilizer. It powers the tractors that harvest crops. It drives the trucks and trains that bring products to market. It heats, lights, and ventilates stores where products are sold. It gets us to the store, to work, to leisure activities.

When oil is cut off (or cut back, which is more likely), as we've all experienced, its price rises. And when oil prices rise, the cost of everything related to oil also goes up. In other words, an oil shortage can produce instant inflation.

"So gold is related to oil through inflation?"

Indeed it is. We were just discussing that the price of gold would go up if there was inflation (even with relatively high interest rates) and if there was also a world crisis. Now combine that with a world crisis that involves oil.

Back in 1982, Britain and Argentina were involved in a crisis involving the Falkland Islands. Gold responded by rising under $10 in value. However, in 1984 the Iran-Iraq War heated up, suggesting it might result in the closure of the Straits of Hormuz, through which about 20 percent of the West's oil passes. This was at a time of very low inflation and relatively high interest rates—both negative factors for gold. However, the addition of an oil crisis was enough to boost gold's price by nearly $40 an ounce in just a few days.

Crisis, inflation, oil—any one of these is enough to boost gold's value. Put any two or all three together and we have the makings of a significant price movement.

"I see what you mean," said George. "But something else disturbs me. I'm just an average person. I only know what I read in the papers. How can I act to take advantage of an oil or other crisis? By the time I get into the market, chances are the price will already have been bid up."

## SUPPLY AND DEMAND

You can be prepared to act, I explained, by getting a handle on gold's long-term trend. If you are aware of supply and demand factors you can already profitably be in the gold market when the unforeseen crisis occurs.

We've already talked about short-term demand caused by a crisis, an oil embargo, or inflation. Long-term supply and demand, however, determine whether gold is slowly trending up or down in price. If we're in a slowly upward trend, then it's profitable to buy gold and let it sit waiting for that unforeseen world event to boost its price. On the other hand, if gold is trending downward, then we're better off out of the market, taking a chance on quickly getting in when a sudden crisis hits. Let's start out with demand.

## JEWELRY DEMAND

What we must understand is that gold has a number of small uses, but only one big use. It's limited uses include

## TIMED BULLION RISKS

electronics (where it's used as a highly conductive material), dentistry (for gold fillings), and as a decorative and reflective covering (as in the ceilings and walls of some buildings). Its biggest use by far, however, is in jewelry. More gold is consumed for jewelry use than for virtually all other uses combined. Hence the old maxim, "As the jewelry market goes, so goes gold."

"You're saying that when jewelry is hot, so too is gold. And when jewelry is not selling, gold's price declines."

It certainly works that way, barring other factors such as we've already discussed. What's interesting is that the jewelry market is highly predictable. During economic expansions when people have money to spend, it does well. But because jewelry is an item easily done without, during recessions when times are hard, people put off such purchases and jewelry demand slackens. Hence during recessions (allowing for a time lag for about nine months after the recession starts), jewelry demand will drop and so will the demand for gold. On the other hand during a recovery (allowing for about a year's time lag), jewelry demand will increase and so will the demand from this source for gold.

"I'm not sure I can agree with that," said George. "Nineteen eighty-four, for example, was at least the second year of a recovery. Yet gold prices were still relatively low. What happened?"

I reminded George that the recovery after the 1981–82 recession was never "across the board." Some sectors recovered; others continued to falter. There were more bank failures in 1984, for example, than during the depths of the recession in 1982. Gold jewelry sales didn't get "hot" then.

In addition, there are the other factors we've discussed. Inflation was also low, below 4 percent; interest rates were high; and except for occasional Iran-Iraq War flare-ups, there were relatively few crises. Although jewelry demand was indeed stronger, it was not as strong as in previous recoveries. That combined with the other factors contributed to keeping gold's value trending down.

"In other words," said George, "because jewelry demand was low and the other factors were negative, it was a bad time to invest in gold."

That's correct, I said. Gold's trend during the second half of 1983 and the first half of 1984 was generally down. That was not a good time to be sitting on the precious metal and waiting for something to happen. There are too many other investments available where profits are possible in the short run.

"But there's another side to this; it's got to be supply," said George. "You can never just trust demand. If supply is way off, it can cause prices to rise even when there is little demand, can't it?"

## THE GOLD SUPPLY

I nodded. Only, I pointed out, gold supplies have been fairly stable over the past several years. South Africa, the world's largest producer, has maintained an almost steady production of about 1,800 metric tons a year. (South Africa is now actually mining greater quantities of lesser grade ore to get the same output.) New gold mining in Canada and other countries has slightly increased overall production. However there have been almost no recent sales from either the International Monetary Fund's huge supply nor the supply of the U.S. The overall picture appears to be that of a stable supply.

## TIMED BULLION RISKS

### THE SUPPLY WILD CARDS

Two wild cards, however, have influenced supply. The first is the Soviet Union. As I mentioned earlier, Russia sells gold to get dollars with which to purchase needed commodities. However, Russian sales are unpredictable. One year it may sell 400 metric tons, the next year only 100. Russian sales appear to depend less on gold market conditions than on internal needs for hard currency.

The other wild card is the huge debt of mainly Third World nations (estimated at more than $600 billion). Some of these nations (including Argentina and Portugal), in order to raise cash to make interest payments on their borrowing from foreign banks, have sold gold. Like Russia's, these sales often have no relevance to the current market conditions.

Supply, therefore, is normally a steady constant; however, it is a constant one cannot count on. Sometimes the supply will remain stable, allowing gold's price to rise. At other times, however, one of the wild cards will enter the market, supplies will increase, and prices will be depressed.

### WHEN TO BUY

George shook his head. "I have to watch out for world crisis, inflation, oil prices, jewelry demand, abundance of supply. Then I have to decide if gold is trending up or down. It seems an impossible task."

I smiled. It seemed impossible to me, too, when I first started. But it really takes only a few minutes each day. I do it in the morning when I read the newspapers (solid business papers like the *Wall Street Journal, New York*

*Times*, or *Los Angeles Times*). All of these factors, every one, are reported in the papers. You'll probably read articles about them frequently.

Now as you read, you can be thinking to yourself, "Does this increased inflation combined with increased jewelry sales mean gold will be trending upward? Is the trend significant? Can I buy now and be ready when a crisis hits?" I asked George if he saw what I meant.

He nodded but then asked, "Why can't I just buy gold when the price is down? Why should I wait until it starts trending upward?"

You can, I said. Many people do just that. They buy gold when its price is relatively low and forget about it. A few years later it takes off in price and they are well positioned. However, that's not the best course for a good investor.

If gold is trending against you, it might go further down after you buy, giving you an immediate loss instead of a profit. Furthermore, if it takes several years for it to turn around, you've lost interest and profits you might have made on that money by sticking it elsewhere. In addition, you've also paid to have the gold stored and insured. George nodded in agreement.

I then repeated the influences that had to be considered in order to maximize the chance for success when buying gold. In other words, buy gold when:

1. Inflation is increasing
2. Interest rates are steady or falling
3. An oil shortage is beginning
4. Jewelry prices and sales are increasing
5. Supplies are steady and there is no gold-dumping by Russia or other countries

## MARKET MANIPULATION

"One last thing about gold," said George. "I've heard that the gold market is sometimes manipulated. Is that true?"
 Probably much less than people imagine, I responded. South Africa undoubtedly does occasionally hold gold off the market to keep the price from falling abruptly. But I doubt any major manipulation can take place. Gold is simply too ubiquitous. (By the way, don't be misled when newspapers report gold's "price-fixing" in London or Zurich or elsewhere. The "fix" merely means the value major buyers and sellers can agree upon.)

## INVESTING IN SILVER

I asked George if he had ever considered investing in silver, pointing out that the profit (and loss) potential were much higher here. It is possible to make far more money more quickly investing in silver than in gold. I saw I had his attention. "Silver is just poor man's gold, isn't it?" he asked.
 Unfortunately, I said, that is a common misconception. It is an error to believe that gold and silver are simply more- and less-expensive versions of the same thing. George asked what I meant.
 I pointed out that while every country recognizes gold as currency, not all do so for silver. Silver is primarily popular in the United States and Asia. The largest "hoarder" of silver is India. Just as families in France keep some gold in their doorposts in case of hard times, those in India keep some silver in the form of jewelry for the same reason.
 However, because silver is less popular worldwide than gold, particularly in the rich Middle East and much of Europe, it does not respond directly to crisis, as does gold. Silver is much less a currency of last resort than gold.

"I don't know." George shook his head. "Every time gold jumps 2 percent in value, silver jumps 5 percent. It seems to me that silver is more sensitive than gold, rather than less."

### SILVER'S VOLATILITY

Yes, it's more volatile, I pointed out. But that's because of the way its price is determined. It's important to understand the kind of market you're up against when you invest in silver.

When we speak of gold's price, we usually mean the "fixed" price of physical gold from the London or Zurich market. When we speak of the price of silver, however, we usually mean the "spot," or current, price on either COMEX (Commodity Exchange of New York) or CBOT (Chicago Board of Trade). In other words, silver's quoted price is rarely the value of the physical metal. Rather, it's the "paper," or spot futures, price. (The physical price is given by several major manufacturers, such as Handy & Harman in New York).

"I don't get it," said George. "What's the difference between 'physical' and 'paper'?"

The difference is day and night, I pointed out. When we talk "physical metal," we're speaking of someone paying cash and taking delivery. That's what happens with gold. When we talk "paper," however, we mean someone leveraging a purchase by putting up only 5 percent of the price or less and almost *never taking delivery.*

"If I read you right," said George, "what you're saying is that because with gold you usually pay cash and get the physical metal it's hard to speculate. But with silver,

—96—

## TIMED BULLION RISKS

because you usually leverage a paper purchase, speculation is far easier."

Yes, that's close, I replied. Gold is many times more expensive than silver, and the buying and selling of the physical metal does dominate the market. (Although you can certainly speculate in gold futures.) With silver, however, we're dealing with a far cheaper commodity, one in which my personal observation is that the paper market dominates. The futures market sets silver's price. Therefore, it's far easier for investors to drive up or down the price of silver by speculating in its futures than to do the same with gold.

George nodded, then asked, "How does that paper market work?"

### SILVER AND THE FUTURE MARKET

The investors (technically referred to as speculators) in the futures market usually make their money by betting the price of a commodity will move up or down. They make a profit when there's price movement *either way*. For the speculators, price movements—having silver quickly move up or down in value—mean profit. Hence, it is to the advantage of speculators to try to force such quick price movements. That's largely why silver is so volatile.

"Boy, it sounds like manipulation to me!" said George.

Some people have claimed that it is, I explained. There have been investigations and at least publicly these have always exonerated the market. However, I think the telling fact is that studies show that fully 85 percent of the people who invest in commodities futures (silver, pork bellies, or

# WEALTH BUILDERS

whatever) lose *all* their money. That means that 15 percent are making out rather well.

"So what you're saying is that, because silver is a commodities game, I should stay out of it unless I happen to be an insider."

That's only partly true, I said. I'm explaining why silver prices are more volatile than gold. I'm also explaining why you're probably better off not getting into the paper silver market. However, if you stay away from the futures market yet stick with *physical silver*, you can actually take advantage of the swings accentuated by the big futures speculators!

## MEDIUM-TERM INVESTMENT

I saw George was keenly interested again. Apparently the thought of using the volatility created by speculators in silver to his own advantage had caught his interest. He had only one question, "How?"

It's not that hard, I replied. Speculators invest in silver short-term. You can invest in it medium-term, under one year. However, before you do, you must first understand the real nature of silver. In my opinion, over the *very long term* it has no investment future.

George looked surprised. I continued. Unlike gold, which has jewelry as its biggest use, silver is an industrial metal. Some is used in electronics, dentistry, and other applications. But by far the major use is in photography. Perhaps 40 percent of all silver is used there.

The problem is that photography is using less and less silver. New processes require less silver in film to get a photographic image. And the explosion in popularity of video cameras and recorders is eroding film's traditional

## TIMED BULLION RISKS

market. Home movies, for example, are rapidly becoming extinct.
    That's the demand perspective, I said. As you can see from the charts, the supply perspective is just as grim. More silver is being mined each year. In addition, as soon as the price reaches about the $10 level, "dishoarding," or the selling of silver in jewelry and other forms, takes place primarily from Asia. As the price struggles to rise, more and more silver comes onto the market. (Even the U.S. government has about 118 million ounces of silver it's waiting to sell as soon as prices rise.)
    That's the bad news, I said. The good news is that in the medium run, silver can be an excellent investment. I could tell that George was really struggling now.

### THE RATIO LEGEND

It has to do with a legend that many investors and even a few economists persist in believing. That legend is called the gold/silver ratio. According to the legend there is an intrinsic relationship between gold and silver. In other words the value of one is linked to the value of the other.
    Back in the 1920s that relationship was roughly 20 to 1. It took $20 to buy 1 ounce of gold or 20 ounces of silver. More recently the "true" ratio was believed to be about 30 to 1.
    The origin of the ratio is ancient. Hammurabi in Babylon spoke of the ratio of silver to gold as being 10 to 1. In more recent times the ratio was kept fairly stable by the fact that the U.S. government set the price of gold at about $35 an ounce. For a long time the value of silver was very roughly $1.10 an ounce; hence the 30-to-1 ratio. (As silver moved up or down that ratio changed, of course.)

**PRICE OF SILVER 1972-1985**

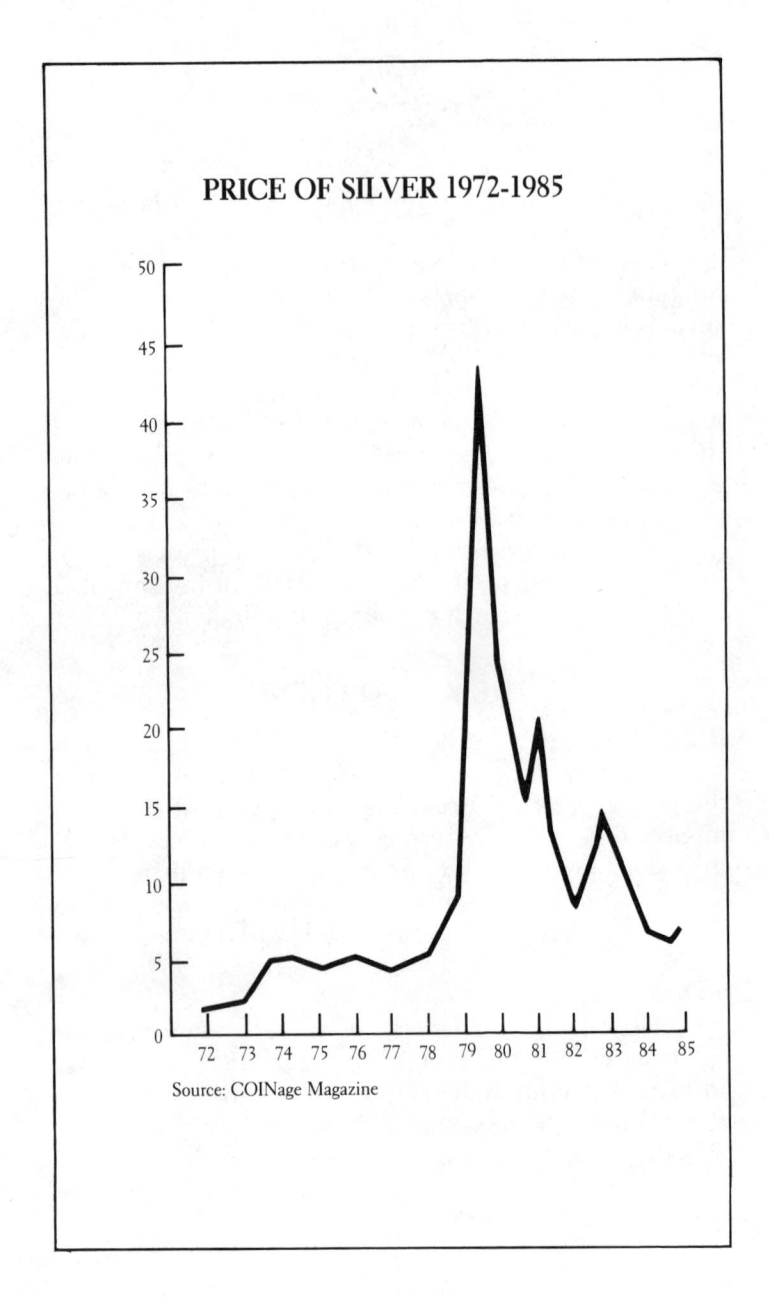

Source: COINage Magazine

# SILVER'S SUPPLY VS. DEMAND 1962-1984

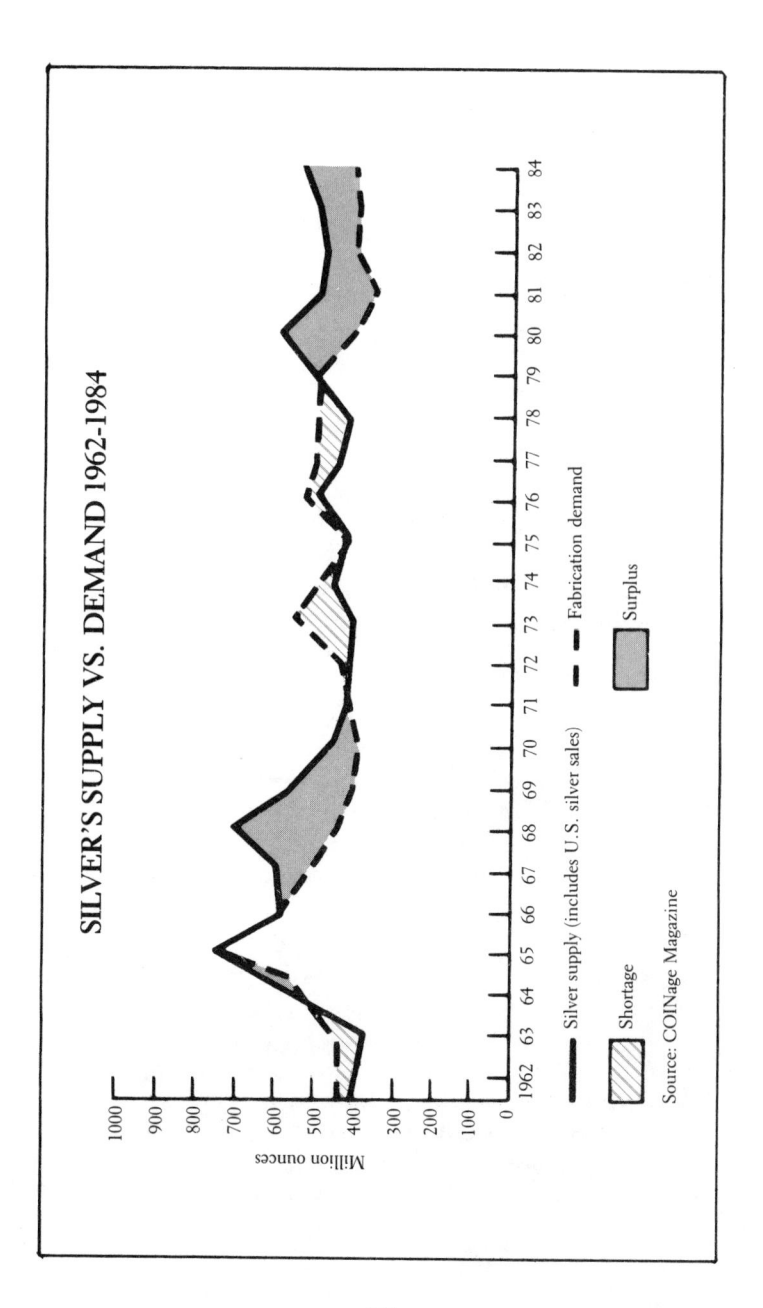

—101—

Over the last few years, however, with the price of gold allowed to float freely, the ratio has gone to a low of 17 to 1 and to a high of 64 to 1. In other words, it has Ping-Ponged all over the place.

Nevertheless, the belief that gold and silver are intertwined persists, and in that belief lies the key to success in silver. A great many investors believe that when gold goes up in price, so too—almost automatically—will silver. Thus, when gold does react to a crisis, inflation or whatever, these investors buy silver. In so doing they create an investment demand which does indeed boost silver's price. This confirms the belief that gold and silver are intertwined, and thus more and more investors pour into silver, rapidly pushing the price higher and higher.

"Does it really work that way?" George was incredulous.

It seems to. Because silver is so much less expensive than gold and because it is more volatile, when market conditions suggest gold is going to go up, some investors turn to silver. Think of it this way. If you buy gold at $400 an ounce and it goes up 5 percent to $420, you make $20. At the same time, silver might be $10 an ounce and might jump 10 percent. For the same $400 you could buy 40 ounces of silver and make $1 on each ounce, or $40. Silver's greater volatility gives you a bigger profit.

## WHEN SILVER LEADS

Of course, silver doesn't always follow gold. In rare instances just the opposite happens: silver pulls gold. That occurred in 1980. At that time, industrial demand for silver was at a peak, and for a number of months there ac-

## TIMED BULLION RISKS

tually was a shortage of silver. This occurred during high inflation when gold was already rapidly rising in prive.

A number of speculators on the various commodity exchanges saw an opportunity to corner the market. They bought silver heavily and demanded physical delivery (as is their right even in a paper exchange). But there happened to be a silver shortage. As the exchanges competed to get silver to fill the orders, the price of physical silver was driven up spectacularly. This caused even more paper speculation and price increases. In a twelve-month period the price of silver rose from $6 an ounce to $50 an ounce! (It rose the last $25 in a matter of weeks.) Silver led the speculation and gold was pulled along.

"That was the time to buy silver!" exclaimed George.

Yes and no, I observed. The time to buy silver was just after it started up; the time to sell was just before it broke.

"But how do you know!" exclaimed George.

By watching closely and waiting. Every so often the conditions are right and prices take off. It could happen again, in the short term, though probably not so spectacularly because there is that big silver surplus.

My belief is to watch gold. When the conditions are right for gold to take off, look to silver. Gold usually gets silver started, and silver's speculative nature often moves it further and faster than gold. But also know when to get out. Understand that silver's rise may *not* be a fundamental upward pressure. It may just be a speculative bubble that will burst in a few weeks or months.

"Right," said George. "I keep track of gold. When the time is right to buy, I make my move. Only instead of gold I buy silver. That's it then. What more do I need to know?"

# WEALTH BUILDERS

Just a little bit, I observed. Remember, it's a gamble. You could lose. Also remember that the last time out you lost your money not so much because of the market but because you were swindled. That is something that you still need to watch out for.

## HOW TO BUY RIGHT

For the investor, buying gold and silver can seem to be a matter of too many choices. First there's the investment vehicle to choose. Should it be coins or ingots? What about mining stocks or commodities futures? Then there's the decision of who to purchase from.

Finally there's the matter of swindlers. The precious metals have their share of "con artists" just like any other field. One of them found you, George.

The real question comes down to criteria. What are the criteria for making a safe precious-metals purchase? I explained to George that he would develop his own criteria over time. Until then, however, there were certain rules I had found which many successful investors followed.

## RULES FOR BUYING GOLD AND SILVER

### 1. Bullion Is Unregulated

*The first and perhaps most important rule to understand is that bullion investment is largely unregulated.* You don't need a license from the Securities and Exchange Commission or the Commodities Exchange Commission to deal in physical gold or silver. (You do need to be registered to trade commodity futures.)

**TIMED
BULLION RISKS**

The fact that a field is not fully regulated by the government, however, does not make it a bad investment arena. It simply means that the old rule of *caveat emptor*, "Let the buyer beware," applies. If you're going to buy physical gold and silver, you need to know who you are buying it from and that the person is an honest dealer.

**2. Know What You Are Buying.**
Most investors today know far more about buying an automobile, for example, than they do about buying bullion. Many who purchase have never before seen a silver ingot or a gold Krugerrand. This means that before we buy we *must* spend some time researching the field. We'd at least look at a house before we'd buy. We'd want to see some background on a stock. Why not get the same type of information when buying bullion?

**3. Never Buy from Someone Who
Insists You Act Quickly or Who
Has a "Special Deal" for You.**
George nodded, this is apparently where he had gotten taken.

Don't be misled by stories of people who have made fortunes overnight in gold and silver. The stories may be true, but you can be darn sure those investors knew what they were buying. Remember, someone who's new to the field won't know a good deal from a bad one. If that's you, how can you tell if a seller really has something special for you?

Also, remember that *there are no bargains in gold and silver*. The last time somebody offered to give a dollar for 95 cents is the last time someone offered to sell gold or silver at discount. Remember, gold and silver are money.

They are never discounted. (The sole exception is gold or silver in the form of bars from unfamiliar fabricators, where it may be discounted for the amount it would cost to have it assayed.)

### 4. Know the Difference Between Physical Gold and Silver and Paper Bullion.

There are many forms and each has its own market characteristics. Physical gold and silver are typically coins and bars. They are the physical metals themselves.

If you buy physical gold and silver outright (you pay the full purchase price in cash), *get delivery* at the time you pay for it.

"But, I didn't want to bother with the cost of insurance and storage. That's why I let that swindler keep my gold in his vault. He said it was like a bank. I thought it was safer."

I nodded sympathetically. I explained that he had been led astray. When we put a thousand dollars in a bank, the bank doesn't actually put one thousand paper dollars in a vault with our name on it. It's just a bookkeeping entry.

On the other hand, when we buy gold or silver and store it, it's not just a bookkeeping entry. The physical gold and silver must actually be put into a vault with our name on it. And therein lies the problem. An error or a theft from a bookeeping entry is difficult to manage, easy to trace. An error or theft of physical gold is as easy as carrying it away, as easy to dispose of as exchanging currency, and almost impossible to trace.

If you want to invest in physical gold and silver, then you must pay the dues the field requires. In this case, those dues are actually storing and insuring the metal yourself. You would never think of buying a car and then handing

## TIMED BULLION RISKS

the car *and title to it* to someone else for safekeeping, would you? George shook his head.
    Then never buy gold and give it to someone else for safekeeping. Store it in your own safety deposit box and for more security, insure it.
    There is one exception. Occasionally a bank will lend money on the purchase of bullion. They may ask that you put up 50 percent of the value, and they will put up 50 percent. As a guarantee of collateral to them, the bank may require holding the metal in its vaults. If it's a reputable bank, this may be an alternative.
    "OK," said George, "that's what I need to look out for. Now, what do I actually buy?"

## WHAT TO BUY IN GOLD

In the past the most common way of buying gold was in the form of Krugerrands, bullion 1-ounce gold coins issued by South Africa. There is a possibility, however, that the Krugerrand may be delegalized in the United States. The reason is that there are many in Congress and elsewhere who are opposed to South African racial policies. As of this writing there are bills in Congress to outlaw the Krugerrand.
    The threat of this action makes the Krugerrand a much less popular coin today. In addition, the fear that if one foreign gold coin is delegalized, others also may be has made gold coins such as the Mexican 50-peso and the Austrian corona less desirable.
    My own feeling is that such fears are largely paranoid. While the Krugerrand may indeed be banned, I don't foresee the country delegalizing all gold ownership (as it did between 1933 and 1975) or outlawing coins other than

the Krugerrand. Alternatives to the Krugerrand are the Canadian maple leaf (1 ounce pure) and the Mexican 50-peso (1.2 ounces).

If you are worried about gold being outlawed, however, I suggest that you invest in old gold, U.S. $20 double eagles. (See the chapter on rare coins for a further explanation.) Because George looked puzzled, I pointed out that it was unlikely the U.S. would delegalize its own currency.

## WHAT TO BUY IN SILVER

"What about silver?" George asked. "You've got me fired up over its possibilities."

There are silver coins (individually and in bags) and silver ingots, I replied. My own feeling is that the best way to invest in silver is in the form of silver dollars.

Silver dollars sell for a premium over the value of the silver in them. You pay extra when you buy, but you get back extra when you sell. The advantage is that there are hundreds, probably thousands, of dealers in silver dollars. There's always a ready market. These coins have liquidity.

"I'd heard that silver bars were the way to go," said George. Actually, I pointed out, there is no standard silver bar (although those offered by Englehard Industries and Handy & Harmon are easily recognized). When it comes time to sell, getting rid of silver dollars is probably the easiest course.

There are also bags. These are canvas bags which contain $1,000 face value of silver coins. Each bag has about 714 ounces of pure silver, and its value is based on the price of silver. I don't like bags for two reasons. The first is the premium on the bags often is too high or too low, it

**TIMED BULLION RISKS**

tends to exaggerate the true market. Secondly, you can never be sure what's in the bag unless you open it. And once it's opened, you may have difficulty getting a dealer to buy it back. All things considered, I'd stay with dollars.

"You mentioned paper gold and silver," chimed George. "How do I invest in those?"

## PAPER GOLD AND SILVER

I pointed out that I had already told George to stay away from these. But just on the outside chance he was interested, he should know something about them. Paper bullion can take many forms. You can buy stock in gold or silver mining companies, you can invest in commodity futures, and you can buy through leveraging. Let's consider each.

### Stock

These are stocks in companies which mine gold and silver. They are offered on the New York, American, and other over-the-counter exchanges. The risk here should be no greater nor any less than when purchasing any other stock. (See the chapter on penny stocks.)

### Commodity Futures

We've already seen that these are extremely speculative and complex investments. You either buy or sell gold and silver, promising delivery of either the purchase price or the commodity at some future date. Enormous leveraging is possible. It is often the case that only 5 to 10 percent of the actual cost of the commodity need be put up. For example, to purchase a contract for $50,000 of silver, only $2,500 may need to be advanced.

The difficulty is that as the investor you're on the hook for the whole $50,000. If prices go the wrong way, you may have to pay far more than your original investment. Bad moves in the commodities market can mean draining your bank account and selling your house and your dog to pay your debt.

I told George to *stay away from commodity futures*. Unless he was an expert, which he was not, he would lose all his money there.

**Paper Leveraging**
A dangerous area is leveraged buying (also sometimes incorrectly called options). Here you commit to make a purchase at some future date for an agreed-upon price, and the seller commits to sell at that price. You have to put up only part of the purchase price (as little as 10 percent). You borrow the balance from the seller, who charges interest. When the sales date arrives, if the price has gone up, you presumably make a profit. If it's gone down, you lose and may have to pay more than the original investment.

The difference between paper leveraging and borrowing on physical gold or silver, as noted earlier, is that with physical gold, you actually secure a bank loan. With paper leveraging the seller makes the loan. In the former, we gain some assurance because, presumably, a bank would never make a loan unless the gold actually were purchased and stored in its vaults. With paper leveraging no such assurance exists.

The best advice I've found is to stay away from paper leveraging. The risk of being taken to the cleaners by an unscrupulous seller is just too great.

"So what you're saying is that for me, the best path would be to buy physical gold or silver, U.S. $20 gold pieces or old silver dollars, right?" I nodded. "Fine, but there's just one last thing. You mentioned there were other precious metals, platinum and palladium. What about them?"

Platinum is a heavy metal used by the automotive industry in catalytic converters. It is also useful as a catalyst in the chemical and petrochemical industries. And it finds uses in the manufacture of glass and as contact points in electronics. Japan is the largest user of platinum, primarily for its auto industry. The U.S. auto industry is also a major user of the precious metal.

Platinum pretty much follows gold. During economic recoveries it tends to go up in price as its industrial use increases. During recession it drops in usage and value.

Palladium is used wherever platinum is used. In addition, it is also used by the dental industry. As with platinum, the largest consumer is Japan.

Palladium's big advantage of late has been its substitution factor. It can be substituted for gold or platinum in both electronic and chemical applications and is far cheaper.

## THE PLATINUM AND PALLADIUM MARKET

I mentioned these two precious metals because of late they have been touted as excellent buys to investors. In some cases they may be. Palladium, for example, showed steady price increases between 1982 and 1985, particularly when the other precious metals were dropping in value. This is because palladium is cheaper and can be substituted for more expensive platinum and gold in many industrial uses.

The great problem, however, is that both platinum and palladium are not liquid investments. It's hard to find a dealer who can sell them to you. It's even harder to find one who will buy them back from you. Most of the play in these two precious metals is on the commodity futures market.

"I'm not trying that," said George. "I think I'll stick with physical gold and silver." I agreed that that was probably a good idea.

## GETTING STARTED

"Let's get started, then," George said eagerly.

Not so fast, I cautioned. Haven't you forgotten something? George looked puzzled.

You need a plan, a *written* plan stating what the conditions are that will get you into the market and get you out.

George shook his head. "I don't need that now that I know it all."

You may indeed know it all, I offered, but unless you write it down, in the heat of investing you may forget or may decide to disregard what you know. Write it down. Write exactly what market conditions have to be for you to enter, what you'll buy, and what market conditions have to be for you to sell.

"Is that really necessary?" George asked.

I told him it could mean the difference between success and another failure.

## INS AND OUTS OF RARE COINS

**RISK**
Moderate

**WHEN TO BUY**
Inflation—low
Interest rates—high

**WHEN TO SELL**
Inflation—high
Interest rate—low to medium

**HOLDING PERIOD**
Long term, 2–10 years

**MINIMUM CASH REQUIRED**
$100

**PROFIT POTENTIAL**
Enormous

**SKILL REQUIRED**
Moderate (good understanding
of field is necessary)

**EFFORT REQUIRED**
May be done as a hobby

**MAJOR DIFFICULTY**
Difficulty determining
true quality of coins

**PROBLEMS**
None foreseeable

# CHAPTER SIX

# INS AND OUTS OF RARE COINS

One of the members of the Future Millionaires' Investment Club, whose name was Howard, expressed interest in rare-coin investing. Howard said he had collected coins as a kid and had heard that there were fortunes to be made today in the field. He wanted to get in on that. "I only have a few hundred dollars to get started with, and I believe this is the place to put it," Howard said.

I pointed out that rare-coin investing had indeed been highly profitable for many people over the years. But it wasn't something you could just jump into without first testing the waters. Investing profitably in rare coins had many secret ins and outs that most outsiders weren't aware of.

"You mean I shouldn't go into the field because I don't have experience?"

I explained that what I meant was that with coins we were dealing with rarities just as if we were buying and selling rare paintings or antiques. That meant that we had to understand the nature of rare items, in this case coins, before we started.

"Is that hard to do?" I saw that I had thrown a scare into Howard. I pointed out that it was not hard to do. It was simply a matter of understanding that investing in coins added a new dimension not found with real estate, stocks, or even bullion—the dimension of rarity. It was not difficult to deal with, once you understood that it was there and had to be tackled.

"In other words I have to know a little bit extra about coins before I invest," Howard said.

Something like that, I replied.

## DETERMINING VALUE IN RARE COINS

As in all investments, I pointed out, we are concerned with buying something at one price and later selling it for a profit. With a stock the procedure is to determine what company is likely to show an increase in value, then go to a broker and buy ten or a hundred or whatever number of shares of that company. Our major decisions are (1) which company to buy and (2) when.

With rare coins, however, we have an additional decision to make. We still must decide: (1) should we buy Mercury dimes or Buffalo nickels? and (2) when should we buy them? But one additional element that is not present with a stock purchase is, (3) *which individual coins(s) should I buy?*

If you get nothing else out of what I'm explaining, I told Howard, this concept now is the one thing to understand. As difficult as it may seem for someone unfamiliar with investing in this field to believe, *each rare coin in the world is virtually different from any other!*

Howard shook his head and almost laughed. "I've got a pocket full of dimes, nickels, and quarters. There are billions of them in circulation and they all look alike. Are you trying to tell me each is unique? They're not; they're all the same."

Not to coin investors and collectors, I pointed out.

## WHICH COINS ARE COLLECTIBLE AS INVESTMENTS?

First off, investment-quality coins are not those in your pocket. For one thing, the fact that they are so plentiful means that they aren't valued for more than what's stamped on their face. As collectors know, for investment we're concerned primarily with *old* coins which haven't been minted for years. In U.S. coins that means the 1700s, 1800s, and very early 1900s. These are coins that usually have been out of circulation for at least fifty years. The vast majority of those originally minted have been lost, destroyed, or melted down. Only a relatively small number remain. Hence their very scarcity makes them valuable.

"Rarity creates value," Howard said. "I can handle that."

That's part of it, I pointed out. The other part is quality. The older coins in your pocket aren't of investment interest simply because they have been banged around and scratched up. Investment-grade coins, on the other hand, are in excellent condition.

"That makes sense," said Howard. "It was just the part about each coin being different from any other that threw me."

Quality, however, gets back to the differences between coins. Howard looked incredulous. "I still can't believe that each coin is different from every other. Even if we talk only about old, rare coins we still have to be talking about thousands and thousands of coins," Howard said.

Think of paintings, I suggested. Van Gogh, Rembrandt, all the masters through the ages created thousands of paintings. Yet, wouldn't you say each one was different?

"Certainly," said Howard. "However each painting was individually crafted. Coins are merely stamped out by a machine."

Yes they are, I agreed, but after they've been taken from the stamping machine, how they've been handled changes them. One coin may have a scratch, another a blemish, yet another a slight thickening of the metal in a spot where it didn't flow quite correctly in the stamping process. Just like fingerprints, the coins are different.

Howard was thoughtful. "Are you saying that every single coin differs so much from every other that you can tell them apart!"

I smiled and replied that technically speaking if we used electronic microscopes that might be possible. For practical purposes, however, under slight magnification it is possible to tell different *grades* of coins.

## COIN GRADING

Some coins look almost exactly as they did when they were minted. Others show greater or lesser degrees of wear. For example, let's take a 1938 Mercury dime (Denver mint). If that coin looks exactly as it did when it came from the mint (assuming it was perfectly struck), it is said to be in *mint state*. To help in determining the quality of coins, the American Numismatic Association (*numismatic* means "coin collecting") has created a grading scale. In this scale the condition of the coin we've just described, the 1938 D

INS AND OUTS
OF RARE COINS

Mercury dime in mint state is the top grade designated as MS-65. A coin which grades as MS-65 is as fine a coin as you can get. (Few coins are ever graded MS-70.)

"In other words it's different from any other coin?" asked Howard.

Technically speaking, it can be different from any other coin. For practical purposes, however, it is in the same condition as any other coin which also grades as MS-65. The grading scale is a convenience to help us make some order out of all the different coins and their different conditions. It sorts them out.

"Are there lots of different grades in the scale?" asked Howard.

I nodded. Let's say our dime has a slight blemish. It's not in quite such fine grade. Now the number value goes down. The next major grade down in value is MS-60. Note we're still using the designation MS. The 60, however, indicates a less fine coin.

Here are the major grades for coins:

    MS-70  (perfect)
    MS-65  (near mint state)
    MS-60
    AU-55  (about uncirculated)
    AU-50
    EF-45  (extremely fine)
    VF-30  (very fine)
    VF-20
    VG-8  (very good)
    G-4  (good)
    AG-3  (about good)

("Proof"—a coin designation—is not a grade but indicates a coin specially manufactured for collectors.)

**WEALTH BUILDERS**

Note that as the coin grades downward both the letter and the number designations change. The number designation refers to the MS grading system we just talked about. The letter designation refers to an older descriptive grading system which is still included for easy reference.

"OK, you've convinced me," said Howard. "Coins are all different. But they are sorted according to their physical condition. Some coins are going to grade high and others low—but so what? What does that have to do with investing? It sounds like something that only an ardent collector would want to know."

Actually, I replied, it's the most basic thing that every investor must know. The single greatest determiner of an individual coin's price is its grade. Grade in coins (in conjunction with rarity) is what determines value.

"It only stands to reason," said Howard, "that a finer coin is going to be worth more than a lesser-grade coin. But what's a few dollars difference? It seems to me the big thing is going to be whether you decide to buy a dime or a quarter, not the grade."

Ah, I thought to myself, the innocence of the new investor. I pointed out that it wasn't just a few dollars difference. For example, here's how our 1938 D Mercury dime prices out according to grade. (I've picked the prices quoted back in 1981 when the market was very strong.)

| VG-8 | F-12 | VF-20 | EF-45 | MS-60 | MS-65 |
|---|---|---|---|---|---|
| $2.50 | $3.25 | $3.25 | $4.25 | $45.00 | $150.00 |

Howard looked amazed. "Are you telling me that the same coin in VG-8 was worth only $2.50, but in MS-65 was worth $150.00? That's an incredible difference!"

I pointed out again that grading is the single biggest

**INS AND OUTS
OF RARE COINS**

determiner of price. Remember that we're dealing in rarities. The basis of this field is not the investor but the *collector*. Collectors always value top condition above all else. Hence, the better the condition, the higher the price.

"I can see that," said Howard. "I imagine that VG-8 coin must have been a real dog. It must have had scratches all over it."

Not at all, I explained. To the average person with an untrained eye it would be difficult to discern the difference between a EF-40 and an MS-65. They'd both look like shiny coins. It would take a knowledgeable investor to tell them apart. Even more to the point, the difference between the MS-60 and the MS-65 grade is even slighter. It would take an *expert* here to tell them apart.

### THE KEY TO COIN INVESTING

"It's impressive," said Howard. "I can see that there's more than meets the eye in rare coins."

Certainly the novice's eye, I countered—which gets to the heart of why we're discussing this at all. Your goal in coin investing is to buy low and resell high. But your ability to do this is directly in proportion to your ability to grade coins. If you buy a coin you believe to be MS-65 grade for $100 and then, a few years later, try to resell for $250, you may find your dreams shattered *if* it turns out the grade was actually MS-60. You could have lost all your profit and instead sustained a loss simply by being off one grade. Being able to accurately grade coins is the key to investing in this field.

"You mean I have to learn how to grade the coins? That could take years!" Howard was incredulous.

If you're going to become a serious investor, yes, to

protect yourself you will have to learn to grade coins. Only it doesn't take years. If you limit yourself to just a few types of coins you can get fairly proficient in a matter of months.

"I don't want to devote that much time to this," said Howard.

There are alternatives, I suggested.

## RELYING ON YOUR DEALER

What many investors do is to find a reputable dealer and rely on that person's ability to grade. Presumably a dealer who has been in the business for many years has the skills to get perfectly graded coins for you.

"How do I find such a dealer?" asked Howard.

Locating a reputable dealer is like trying to find any other reputable merchant. The three R's are always a good guide:

**1.** *Reputation.* What do other dealers and investors say about this person? What does the Better Business Bureau and the District Attorney's Office have to say about him?

**2.** *Repeat business.* Does this dealer have a satisfied clientele who repeatedly go back to him?

**3.** *Reliability.* How long has the dealer been at the same location? (The longer the better.) Will the dealer guarantee the merchandise (take it back and refund your money if it isn't as he says it is).

"Can you name some dealers I can go to?"

## INS AND OUTS
## OF RARE COINS

I can, I replied, but I won't. Instead I suggest you do a little homework and find out those who are the best in your city. A good place to start are the publications in which dealers advertise. The three that you need to check out are:

*COINage*, the largest circulation coin and bullion magazine in the world. 17337 Ventura Blvd., Encino, CA 91360.

*Coin World*, the weekly newspaper of the coins field. Amos Press Incorporated, Box 150, Sidney, OH 45365.

*ANA Bulletin*, the official publication of the American Numismatic Association. 818 N. Cascade, Colorado Springs, CO 80903.

"So what you're saying is that by relying on my dealer, I can do just as well as if I were an expert myself."

No, not really I replied. Being your own expert is best. The reason is that grading is a very subjective thing. One reputable dealer, in his opinion, may grade a coin MS-65. Another reputable dealer who happens to be a harsher grader may grade that same coin only MS-60. The difference in grading can be an honest difference of opinion. That difference, however, can be the difference between profit and loss for you.

What many investors do is to pick one dealer and establish a relationship with him. You buy the coins from him and later sell them back. A reputable dealer won't change a coin grade he himself made a few years earlier. Your danger here is that the dealer might go out of business.

## CERTIFICATES

"Isn't there any final authority?" Howard asked.

I smiled. I explained that Howard was suffering from a mental syndrome called paper credibility. In the past you've invested in stocks or real estate or whatever, and you've always received a piece of paper to prove the value of what you bought. With stocks it was the stock certificate. With real estate it was the deed. Now with coins you want the same thing, a piece of paper attesting to the value of the coin. As it turns out, such paper credibility is available.

ANACS (American Numismatic Association Certification Service) provides authentication and grading of coins for a fee. They will examine coins sent to them and issue a certificate which includes a photo of the coin as well as a statement that it is authentic (not counterfeit) as well as to what its grade is. (ANACS is located at 818 N. Cascade, Colorado Springs, CO 80903.) If you want paper credibility, that's the way to go.

"Sounds great," said Howard. "Obviously that's the right approach to take. How can anyone argue with a certificate?"

It's possible, I said. Remember, the people at ANACS are only human. They do the best job they can, but they handle thousands of coins a month and they are issuing only an opinion as to the condition of a coin at the time they saw it. The coin could have been damaged since its examination, or even a lower grade coin substituted with the certificate.

"Wow," said Howard, "I can't imagine anyone doing that."

INS AND OUTS
OF RARE COINS

Remember we're dealing with rarities not bookkeeping entries. There are unscrupulous people who will try to cheat those who are unaware. Your best guarantee remains your own expertise in grading coins and, barring that, the expertise of an honest dealer.

## COUNTERFEITS AND "SLIDERS"

"Is there a big problem in bad coins?" Howard looked concerned.

No, not big I answered. But as a doctor once told me when I was having a cancer exam, "The chances of your having it are 1 in 100. But if you're the one, the odds don't mean anything." (It turned out I was fine.) There are two big areas to be careful of in rare coins, counterfeits and "sliders."

Counterfeits are fake coins created to appear to be rare originals. We don't usually find counterfeits until we get into coins valued at many thousands of dollars. It's simply a matter of economics for the counterfeiter. Why go to the time, expense, and trouble of counterfeiting a $100 coin when with the same effort you can work on a $10,000 fake. Expert dealers normally can spot a fake a mile away.

Sliders are a bigger problem. These are coins which are in between grades. As we've seen, the higher the grade, particularly at the top end, the more valuable the coin. What is a dealer to do when he has a coin which is better than MS-60, but not as good as MS-65? To solve this dilemma, middle grades have come into existence. There are now MS-62 and MS-63 coins.

The problem occurs in deciding whether to say an in-between coin is MS-60 or MS-62 or MS-63. Just one

—125—

number difference can make a big change in the coin's price. The natural tendency for anyone is to "slide" the coin up to the higher number. It takes a very honest dealer and investor to put an MS-60 designation onto a coin that just might slide up to MS-62.

When you're involved in rare coins for a while you'll find that there are all kinds of creative reasons given for sliding coins. The best rule of thumb to follow, however, is to *always assume the coin is the lowest possible grade.* That's your best bet to avoid getting hurt.

I saw Howard was listening intently. He said, "I've learned a lot about coins, but I still don't know how one makes money in the field. Do I just go out and buy anything I can afford?"

## HOW TO MAKE MONEY IN RARE COINS

There are basically two ways to make money in rare coins, I told Howard. The method you choose depends on your degree of involvement in the field. Let's begin with the method you're *least* likely to select. This involves full-time work and requires that you become an expert. This is the "discovery method."

The discovery method involves going to dealers to examine their coins, appearing at coin auctions (which are held constantly all around the country), talking with investors who want to sell their coins. This is done with the goal of discovering coins which are underpriced. Perhaps a dealer has an 1840 large cent with a small date on it. The value could be $65. But you notice that the 18 in the date is a bit larger than the rest of the numbers. This is a specific

## INS AND OUTS OF RARE COINS

variety worth almost twice the price of the other coin. You make the purchase, correctly identify the coin, and resell for an immediate profit.

Or perhaps you find a coin an investor has incorrectly graded too low. You buy and quickly resell for a profit. Or maybe you're aware that there's a sudden big demand for "liberty head" quarters (issued between 1892 and 1916). You've learned this because you been following the *Grey Sheet*, which gives the latest coin prices (*Grey Sheet, Coin Dealer Newsletter*, P.O. Box 2308, Hollywood, CA 90028), or because you've seen many purchase requests on the teletypewriter that connects dealer to dealer.

You find someone who isn't aware of this sudden demand. You buy the coins cheap and turn around and sell them for a profit. In other words, you're playing the middleman game. You win because you've spent enough time to get the latest and best information.

"That's not for me," said Howard. "I can't afford to devote my life to coin investing."

I understand, I said. You're more likely to profit by the second method.

### BUY AND HOLD

The easiest way to make a profit in coins is to buy and hold. Making a profit here is almost guaranteed, if you have patience.

"It sounds too easy," said Howard. "You mean I just go out and purchase some coins, then wait for them to go up in value?"

Not exactly, I replied. A lot depends on knowing *when* to buy and sell. There are some promoters and dealers who will suggest that *now is the time to buy!* Now turns out to be *always;* in other words, whenever they are trying to sell.

The truth is that there are good times to buy and bad times. The reason is that the rare coin market is *cyclical.* It operates on the basis of cycles, the peaks and valleys of which are miles apart. The easiest way to make a profit on coins is to identify a valley in the cycle and buy, then wait for a peak (which could be several years away) and sell. Coins have been moving in cycles for longer than anyone has kept track. To get an idea of a recent cycle here is an index of coin prices compiled by *COINage* magazine.

This index shouldn't be taken as gospel. It traces only twenty key coins. But over the years it has proven to be a generally good indicator of the field. Note how the most recent cycle peak was in 1980 and how the most recent valley was in 1982. This chart *suggests* that we are once again building toward a new high at some undetermined time in the future.

"That's great because it's easy," said Howard. "Only how can I be sure when we're at the bottom of a cycle and I should buy, or at the top and I should sell?"

## THE EASY METHOD

There's an easy answer and a complex answer to that, I replied. The easy answer is this: We're at or near the bottom of a cycle when no one wants to buy coins and everyone wants to sell. We're at or near a peak when everyone is excited about coins and is telling you it's the perfect place to put your money. In other words, the general public (also known as the "dumb money") always enters the cycle at the wrong time. Find out what the public is thinking and do the opposite.

# LONG TERM PRICE INDEX

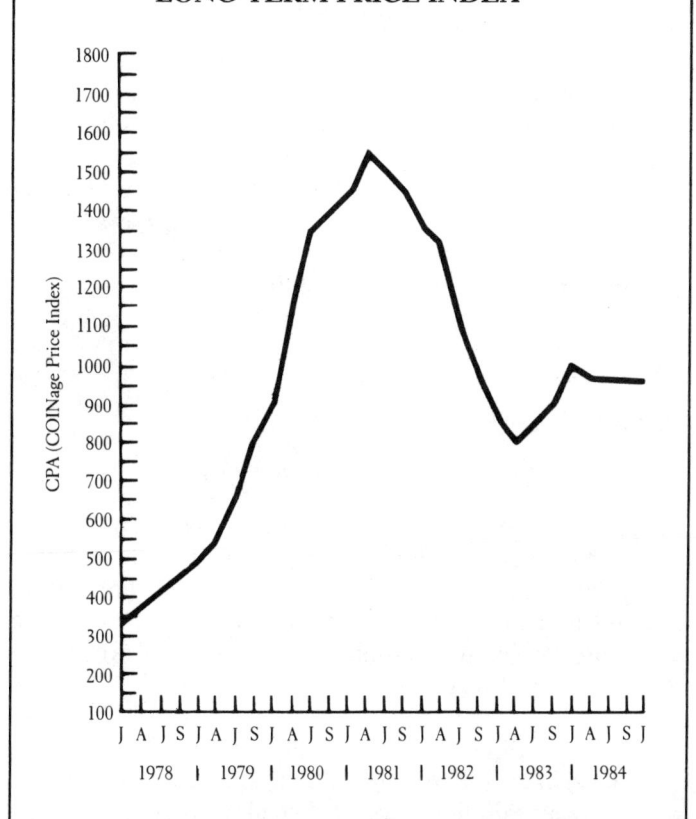

Index of rare coin prices based on COINage Magazine's CPA listing of 20 key coins. Chart lists index by Jan., April, July and Sept. dates.

## THE COMPLEX METHOD

The complex method of finding the peaks and valleys is to understand what causes the cycle. That is basically inflation and interest rates. Just as bullion is seen as an inflation hedge, so too are rare coins. In times of steep or rapidly rising inflation, investors turn to rare coins. During periods of moderate or low inflation, they stay away. This action, of course, is tempered by interest rates. High interest rates provide an attractive risk-free alternative. Consequently, if interest rates are higher than inflation, rare coins will probably not be doing well. If they're lower, the coins will fare better. (See Chapter Five on bullion for a more detailed explanation.)

## THE ROLE OF ANTICIPATION

Finally there's the matter of anticipation. Coin prices move up rapidly when inflation is *anticipated,* often long before that inflation occurs. On the other hand, they are slow to respond to a lowering of inflation. Investors keep holding on to their coins hoping that inflation will get worse and the coin market better.

"What you're saying, then," said Howard, "is that rare coins are inflation and interest rate sensitive."

I nodded and explained that like all other investments today, liquidity was the real challenge. (Reread Chapter Three for a description of the liquidity challenge.)

"OK," said Howard, "right now inflation happens to be very low and interest rates very high, so it's the right time to buy, correct?"

Remember anticipation, I said. *The market moves up quickly, down slowly.* If inflation has just gone down or if

## INS AND OUTS
## OF RARE COINS

rates have just gone up, it may take many months, perhaps a year or more, for the market to react.

"Nevertheless," said Howard, "I've determined it's time for me to buy. Which coins specifically should I buy?"

## WHAT TO BUY

That's easy, I replied. For you as a part-time, long-term investor it doesn't matter what you buy, within certain parameters. Here's what those limits are:

1. *Buy American coins or ancients (Roman).* These have tended to lead the field and hold their value more than other coins. Stay away from modern foreign coins. The market for them is sporadic.

2. *Buy older coins.* For U.S. denominations, remember that coins prior to 1900 are the best. Stay away from recent issues that appear to be popular. Their popularity may wane just as quickly as it blossomed.

3. *Buy only MS-60 or higher grade.* This provokes more arguments than anything else. These top-grade coins are expensive, often too expensive for many investors. I can recall one conversation I had in 1978 with an investor who had $500 to spend. She could afford one MS-60 coin or seven EF-40 coins. "Why should I buy only one top-grade coin when I can start a collection of lower-grade pieces?" she wanted to know. She disregarded my advice and bought more of the lesser quality coins.

We were on the upswing of a coin market cycle and prices took off. By 1980 her $500 if invested in one MS-60 coin would have been worth $4,000. On the other hand, the combined value of the seven lower-grade coins she bought for $500 had risen to only $900. Yes, she made a

## WEALTH BUILDERS

profit, but she missed out on a far bigger profit by not buying the top grade. Top-grade coins always move up faster than lower grades. (Unfortunately, they also tend to hold their value longer, making them very difficult to purchase.)

  4. *Try to buy similar coins.* A collection of coins often will sell for more than individual pieces (unless the pieces are extremely rare). Get started buying all the Mercury dimes (by date and mintmark) or one of each denomination of a coin for a particular year. Some investors will pay a premium for a full collection.

### HOW MUCH DO I NEED TO GET STARTED?

Howard asked the question, and I quickly replied that there's no minimum amount. Coins can be bought for almost any price. The most expensive are near the million dollar range. The least expensive even in top grade can be under $100. Just pick a spot within the parameters just discussed, and if the timing is right go to it.

### WHAT ABOUT GOLD COINS?

Gold coins are collected just as are silver and copper ones. In rare coins the rarity often boosts the price so high that the value of the gold in the piece is often just a fraction of the total cost. Nevertheless, in general, gold coins do sell for more than other ones. Recently, common date, less than top-grade gold $20 (double eagles) have been going up dramatically in price as investors in bullion have switched out of Krugerrands, which might be delegalized. (See Chapter

# INS AND OUTS OF RARE COINS

Five on bullion.) Fortuitous circumstances can always boost the value of a coin at unexpected times.

## WHAT ABOUT STORAGE?

Like bullion, coins do not yield interest. They cost you to keep them because you must put them in a safe place (usually a safe deposit box), and you should carry insurance on them. Because rare coins are a long-term investment, you should weigh your action carefully in becoming involved with them over some other shorter-time, higher-yield investment.

"I'm ready for rare coins," said Howard. "Thanks for the information. I'm going right out and buy some."

## WRITE OUT YOUR PLAN

Haven't you forgotten something? I asked. What about your plan?

Howard shook his head. "I don't need a plan. I've got all the knowledge now."

Nevertheless, I pointed out, in six months you might forget what you've learned here. It's best to write down exactly what the conditions are for your getting into coins, what you're planning to buy, and what the conditions are for your selling.

The latter is most important. It avoids the temptation to hold too long, to wait until the peak has passed and prices are nose-diving before you sell.

## OPTIONS FOR THE DARING INVESTOR

**RISK**
High

**WHEN TO BUY**
Anytime market is moving

**WHEN TO SELL**
Anytime market is moving

**HOLDING PERIOD**
Short

**MINIMUM CASH REQUIRED**
$200–$300

**PROFIT POTENTIAL**
Enormous

**SKILL REQUIRED**
Moderate (good understanding
of field is necessary)

**EFFORT REQUIRED**
May be done as a hobby

**MAJOR DIFFICULTY**
Quiet market can destroy this investment

**PROBLEMS**
None foreseeable

# CHAPTER SEVEN

# OPTIONS FOR THE DARING INVESTOR

The first words from Joan were, "I'm a gambler and I want a gambler's investment."

She was a member of the Future Millionaires' Investment Club and she had a determined set to her jaw. "I like playing at Las Vegas and Atlantic City. I'm not afraid to risk my money, as long as I can see the possibility of a big payoff. I'm not asking for a sure bet, but I want something with a little challenge to it."

I knew that some people likened investing to gambling, but I hadn't seen many who were so blunt about it. I said that there were many avenues she could take which would give her great leverage, huge potential profits and, unfortunately, high risk.

## BIG RISKS IN COMMODITIES FUTURES

I pointed out all investing is like gambling, but that the commodities futures market is perhaps the area of greatest risk. There the investor puts up only 5 percent or less of the investment price and gambles on whether a commodity will go up or down in value. If you are right you can quickly make millions.

However, in good conscience, I can't recommend the

futures market to any but the most seasoned investor. The reason is that studies that I've seen indicate that as many as 85 percent of all investors in futures lose all the money they put up. The odds against winning are just too great.

## THE OPTIONS MARKET

However, I pointed out, there is an alternative and that is options. In recent years the options market has opened up considerably. There are options on real estate, on stocks, and, more recently, on some commodities, such as gold. An option is still a gamble, but the amount risked can be small and there is a limit to the amount you can lose. (In a commodities futures investment, you potentially can lose twenty times or more the amount you originally invested!)

Joan thought about it for a moment, then replied, "All right, I'll try options. What are they?"

"Options are a high-risk investment," I warned, pointing out that she might like options and, then again, perhaps they wouldn't be quite her cup of tea. It is first necessary to learn something about them. The easiest way to learn about options is to see how they are used in real estate.

## REAL ESTATE OPTIONS

I pointed out that most people are familiar with a real estate option. Suppose an investor buys an option on a piece of property. That means that up until a certain time limit, *the investor has the right, but not the obligation* to purchase the property for a set price. For example, I might pay you $500 for the option to purchase your home within ninety days for $100,000.

## OPTIONS FOR THE DARING INVESTOR

I could exercise my option, in which case I'd have to come up with the $100,000 within the time limit. Or I could let my option go, in which case I don't have to buy your house. In that case I am out no more than my $500.

"Why not just buy the house outright?" asked Joan. "Why bother with the $500 option money?"

For good reasons, I replied. Sometimes it's to our advantage to tie up a property without putting a lot of money into it. This is particularly the case in a rapidly rising market as occurred in the late 1970s. Then some investors would tie up a dozen houses for a year's time on options. (At $500 per option their total investment was only $6,000.) Because it was a rapidly rising market, the houses were usually worth thousands more apiece at the end of the year. Now the investor could buy for the previously set low price and resell for the then-current higher value. I knew of one investor who for two years bought a house a week in this fashion. At the end of that time he had amassed a small fortune.

"But the real estate market's not booming right now," said Joan. "Can this options play work in a quiet market?"

It can, I pointed out, but it takes much longer and it is more difficult. In any event, real estate just serves as a useful example. The real opportunities in options today are probably in the stock market. Joan nodded, "I'm ready to play the stocks."

### STOCK OPTIONS

Stock options work in a fashion similar to real estate options. However, with stocks you can purchase either an option to buy (stock within a set date) or an option to sell (stock within a set date). A buy option is called a *call* and a sell option is called a *put*. The whole field is sometimes referred to as puts and calls.

Joan shook her head. "Sounds complicated."

It's not that bad, I replied. Sometimes when we hear new terms we tend to think they refer to complex subjects. But that's not the case here. "Call" simply means your right to "call for," or buy, a stock. "Put" simply means your guarantee to "put up," or sell, a stock. Perhaps an example will help.

## BUYING CALLS

We'll take an actual stock from the Big Board, Coleco Industries, and two actual years, 1982 and 1983. At the beginning of 1982, Coleco was selling for about $11 a share. To buy 100 shares would cost $1,100 plus commission.

Now, let's say that instead of buying 100 shares for $1,100, we instead bought options. Options are usually sold in $5 intervals up to $50. $10 intervals up to $100, and $20 over $100. That is, we could get an option to buy Coleco at $10 or $15 or $20 or $25, and so forth.

"I don't get it," said Joan. "What do you mean we could 'get' an option to buy?"

We could purchase a call (the right to buy) option at, for example, $20. That means that we have the right but not the obligation to buy Coleco at the price of $20 a share.

"Doesn't make sense," said Joan. "Coleco is selling at $11. Why would we want to buy at $20?"

We would want to buy at $20 a share, I explained, if we thought that Coleco was going to go up in value. If we thought, for example, that Coleco would go from $11 to $30, we might buy a $20 call. The $20 would be our *striking price*, or the price at which we would be "in the money."

## OPTIONS FOR THE DARING INVESTOR

Let's say that we had a call (100 shares) at $20 and Coleco moved to $30. We're in the money for $10 a share. We have 100 shares, so our call has an "intrinsic value" of $1,000.

"I still don't get it," said Joan. "Why would anyone sell us a call at $20 when the price had gone to $30?"

### DETERMINING VALUE

Time, I pointed out. Time is the great element of options. Options are sold for three months at a time. We might buy a three-month, six-month, or nine-month option on Coleco. When we bought our $20 call, the price might only be $11. It's easy to see why someone would sell this to us since we're agreeing to buy a stock for $9 a share more than it's worth. However, if we held onto it for six months and it turned out to be worth $30 a share, then the intrinsic value of the option would be worth $10 a share *plus* its time value. We would make $10 a share.

"That depends," said Joan, "on what we paid for the call option. If we paid $100, then we made a $900 profit plus time value. But if we paid $1,000 for it then we haven't made a dime."

### INTRINSIC VALUE

Quite right, I pointed out. The option price is a critical factor. It is determined by three things. The first is the *intrinsic value* of the option. If the option is in the money, then it is automatically worth at least the difference between the call price and the actual price of the stock (plus any time value). If the call price is $20 and the actual price $30, then the intrinsic value is $10 a share (100 shares are worth $1,000). If the call price is $20 and the actual price is $10, then the intrinsic value is zero. (The stock is said to be "out of the money.")

"You mean the call is free?" asked Joan incredulously.

## THE VALUE OF TIME AND VOLATILITY

No, I replied. I said the intrinsic value was zero. But there's also a time value and a volatility value (we'll get to the latter in a few moments). If the call has six months to go, then there's always the hope that the stock might go up in six months. That hope is worth something.

The longer the time before the expiration of the option the greater the hope that prices might go up (or down, as the case might be). The shorter the time, the less hope. Consequently, even a call option which is out of the money (or has no intrinsic value) will have some time value depending on how long it has until its expiration date. Let's go back to our Coleco example.

When we get our call option, Coleco is selling for $11 a share. We buy a call for $20 a share. We are $9 out of the money, so the option has no intrinsic value.

But it is October and we buy a six-month option. We have until March of the next year, six months hence, before that option expires. We can hope that during that six months Coleco stock will move toward $20 (our striking price) and beyond, putting us in the money.

Let's say that the value of this hope costs $100. That means that the price of a call option is $100. (For convenience we're going to overlook options commissions for the rest of this example.) We have $1,100 to spend. We can either buy 100 shares of Coleco outright for $1,100, or we can buy 11 call options at a striking price of $20 for $1,100.

Finally, there's volatility. The value of the option depends also on the volatility of the underlying stock. A stable stock like General Motors is unlikely to have much volatility value. A highly fluid stock like Coleco is likely to have great volatility value.

Joan nodded, "It looks like you'd have far greater leverage with the call options. Provided the stock goes up."

## THE RISK AND THE ADVANTAGE

I agreed. You've hit upon the advantage and the risk of the option. If we buy 11 call options, we control 1,100 shares of stock. We've increased our leverage by a factor of 11. However, if Coleco never gets to our striking price and we hold our option to expiration, we could lose our entire investment of $1,100. (Remember, six months hence when time runs out, there is no time premium.)

On the other hand, if we bought the actual stock, we would always still have its value. If after six months Coleco was still at $11, then we could sell and not have lost a dime.

"So what you're saying," said Joan, "is that if you buy the stock you have greater security. But if you buy the option you give up the security for leverage."

That's correct, I replied, given our use for the option. (There are other uses which will be described later.)

"OK," she said, "but what's the payoff?"

Since we chose Coleco, let's consider the actual payoff that would have occurred roughly during the time frame we're considering, Coleco moved from $11 a share to over $60 a share. Here's how our option investment looks just before the expiration date:

### A CALL EXAMPLE

Purchased 11 calls
(1,100 shares)
Our cost = $1,100

Striking price
$20 (× 1,100 shares = $22,000)

Current price
$60 (× 1,100 shares = $66,000)
Difference = $44,000

Our profit = $44,000
−$1,100 (our investment)
=
$42,900

---

"Are you telling me," Joan demanded, "if I had bought 11 Coleco call options in 1982 for $1,100, that six months later I could have shown over $40,000 in profit?"

Pretty close, I said. You bought the right to purchase but not the obligation at $20. The stock zoomed to over $60. You made $40 a share profit and you had control of 1,100 shares.

"Wait a minute." Joan sounded as if she had found the thread to unravel the whole example. "I still needed the money to buy the stock at the end of the option period. I still needed the $22,000 in this case. Where would I get that?"

You wouldn't have needed it, I explained. You don't need to exercise your option to get the money out (al-

## OPTIONS FOR THE DARING INVESTOR

though you can). You do have to sell the option, however. In simple terms, your broker handles the entire transaction for you, and you get your profit without ever having put up the money to buy the actual shares of stock.

"My gosh," said Joan, "this is what I've been waiting for. All I have to do is pick a stock that's going to go up in value and I can get rich."

Picking the right stock is, of course, the trick, I replied. Remember, it has to move within the time frame you've chosen. But it's not necessary that it only go up in price. You can buy a put option (the right but not the obligation to sell) for the same stock.

### BUYING PUTS

"I don't follow." Joan looked puzzled again.

A put simply means that you agree to sell stock. Let's say that, after you had taken your profit on Coleco, with some of your profits you bought 50 Coleco puts at $50. Remember the stock was then worth $60 a share. You're buying the right *but not the obligation* to sell Coleco stock at $50. In this case, you're buying 50 put options, or you're controlling 5,000 shares.

"But, I don't own 5,000 shares," Joan said worriedly. "How can I sell something I don't own?"

This is sometimes the most difficult concept for individuals who are entering options to grasp, but if you stick with it you should be able to figure it out. A put is just the opposite of a call. With a call you had the right but not the obligation to buy. Remember, you didn't actually buy the 1,100 shares of stock to make your profit. You never actually exercised the option. You instead got rid of it for just the profit. The same holds true for a put. If you're in the money, you can simply sell your option for the profit and put that in your pocket. You never have to own the 5,000 shares of stock.

Joan still looked puzzled.

If you have trouble with this, then simply don't buy put options. Just stick with call options. Almost always, however, once an investor gets close to the actual market, the operation of puts becomes clear.

Joan nodded and said, "I think I understand. Go ahead. What happens if I bought 50 puts?"

The stock was at $60; your striking price was at $50. You're $10 out of the money. We'll say the options cost you $100 apiece (the option premium isn't a set price but varies enormously in actual practice). Your total investment is $5,000.

Between early 1983 and about September of 1983 Coleco dropped in value to about $20 a share. Here's what your profits would have looked like:

---

### A PUT EXAMPLE

Purchased 50 puts
(5,000 shares) Cost $5,000

Striking price $50

Value of stock $250,000

Current price $20

Value of stock $100,000

Profit = $150,000 less
$5,000 investment = $145,000

---

## OPTIONS FOR THE DARING INVESTOR

In this case, you had the *right* to sell at $50 a share. But by the time it was close to expiration for your option, the stock was selling on the open market for only $20 a share. In theory, therefore, you could now buy 5,000 shares for $20 a share and then exercise your right to *sell* them at your striking price of $50 a share, pocketing $30 a share, or $150,000, in profits.

"Wowee!" said Joan. "This is better than Las Vegas. Where do I get the chips!"

It was better, I said, because things worked out to your advantage. It doesn't always work that way. What it takes to work are the three ingredients: intrinsic value, time, and volatility. What you want is a stock that rapidly goes up and/or down in price. What will kill you is a stock that has no movement.

For our example, I chose Coleco Industries which was probably the most volatile stock on the entire New York Stock Exchange for that period of time.

### STRADDLES

Since you're interested only in volatility, many times investors will purchase a *straddle*. If the stock is currently valued at $20, they might buy a call at $25 and a put at $15. Now, when the stock moves $5 in value *in either direction*, they are in the money. Here is an example of a typical straddle:

| | |
|---|---|
| Call striking price | $25 |
| Current value | $20 |
| Put striking price | $15 |

"According to this example," said Joan, "the stock has to

move only $5 to get me into the money. That's better than the other example with Coleco. There the stock had to move $10 before I was in the money."

True, I replied. But the hypothetical premium on the Coleco example was only $100 for each option. When the striking price is closer to the actual value, the premium increases. It might be $300 an option given the distance to your striking price. On the other hand, if the striking price is further away, the option might cost a lot less.

## WHEN TO BUY

"The key to all of this," said Joan, "comes back to picking the right stock."

Yes, I replied, and the right time for the right stock. Options make sense in a volatile market. When the market is moving rapidly *up or down* in price, you can make money in options. When it is stagnant, you don't want to be in options.

It's interesting to relate this to inflation and interest rates. The stock market is highly sensitive to both factors. Just the threat of higher inflation or interest rates can send stocks plunging. On the other hand, lower inflation and a drop in interest rates can move stocks up.

"In other words, I should watch the stock market trends?" asked Joan.

Yes, it's vital to watch trends. But it's equally important to watch individual stocks.

## WHAT TO BUY

You want to watch the leaders at the moment. For our example I picked Coleco. At the time it was rising in value,

## OPTIONS FOR THE DARING INVESTOR

high-tech stocks (particularly those involving computers) were hot. At the time it fell, the bloom was off high-tech computer stocks. While Coleco may have led, the whole industry tended to follow.

Next time it may be pharmaceuticals or consumer goods or oil stocks. You want to identify which stocks are hot. Then you want to follow several individual stocks to see how they are performing. (See Chapter Nine on penny stocks for hints here.)

What I do is to have my stockbroker help me select stocks which have shown great volatility over the past twelve months. Then I write to the companies for information. Finally, I chart their day-to-day progress. I try to identify what's made them volatile and what factors might cause their prices to become volatile in the future. All this *before* I invest a dime.

### WHERE TO BUY

Stock options are available from any stockbroker. Even the discount brokers offer them. Simply walk into a stockbroker's office and say you want to buy a stock option. The broker can sell it to you on the spot. (But remember, not all stocks have options available on them.)

### THE RISK

"You're saying that if I spend the time, I can make this a safer investment?" asked Joan.

No, I replied. Options can only be considered high-risk. You pay your money and you take your chance. It's very much like gambling. Studying the market can, however, help you to make an educated guess.

## WRITE IT DOWN

Before you get in, however, you should have a plan of attack. Write down the names of stock you're going to buy options on. Determine how much you'll spend, how long you'll stay in, and when you'll get out if the market goes the other way. Decide whether you're going to buy puts, calls, or straddles. Write down exactly how much you can afford to lose, and don't invest a dime more.

## OTHER USES FOR OPTIONS

Sometimes investors will hedge a position with an option. They will buy a stock, then get a put against it. If the stock goes up in price, they can always sell it. If it goes down, the put protects them against loss.

In other cases investors will use a *spread* or even write their own options, both of which are more sophisticated ploys. For additional information on options, check with any broker and ask for the booklets (usually free) put out by the Chicago Board of Options. They are highly informative.

## OPPORTUNITIES IN TAX SALES

**RISK**
Moderate to high

**WHEN TO BUY**
Anytime

**WHEN TO SELL**
Inflation—high
Interest rates—low to medium

**HOLDING PERIOD**
Long-term

**MINIMUM CASH REQUIRED**
$100

**PROFIT POTENTIAL**
High

**SKILL REQUIRED**
Moderate (good understanding
of field is necessary)

**EFFORT REQUIRED**
May be done one or two days a month

**MAJOR DIFFICULTY**
Locating and traveling to tax sales,
later disposing of property

# CHAPTER EIGHT

# OPPORTUNITIES IN TAX SALES

Jim was a new member of the Future Millionaires' Investment Club. He had joined for reasons other than those expressed by the other members I had spoken with.

"I'm tired of keeping my money in a bank money market account. To begin with, I don't have a whole lot, and the interest on what I've got isn't ever going to make me rich. I want a way to get into an investment field and make a killing!"

I thought a while about what Jim wanted. He was after quick bucks, and it sounded as though he might be willing to spend a little bit of his time getting it. I asked him if he could devote one or two days a month to an investment *if* he could see that it was making him lots of money.

"Two days?" he exclaimed in his big booming voice. "I'll spend two weeks if that's what it takes!"

I said that a few days well spent would be enough, but he had to use his time wisely. I suggested that he become involved in one of the oldest methods of making money—buying real property at tax sales.

## WHY TAX SALES?

Jim shook his head. "I don't know about that. It sounds like I'd be making money off someone else's misery. I'm not sure I'd want to get involved."

## WEALTH BUILDERS

I pointed out that I wasn't speaking of buying property *from a person who was losing it*. I was speaking of buying property from government agencies. These agencies frequently took back property which was abandoned or whose owners had died with no heirs. I pointed out that in this day and age, precious little property was lost simply because an alert, active owner didn't pay the taxes. Property was too valuable for that. Usually there were special circumstances.

I then told Jim about my father. This was back in the late 1940s. Our family had survived the Great Depression and then the Second World War. We were a great family, but in terms of material posessions, we had very little.

My father wanted to buy a house for the family. During the war he had been too old to get into the service and so had worked in a defense plant. He had managed to save up $3,000. That wasn't a whole lot with which to buy a house, even in those days, and he didn't have the GI Bill to help him.

He spent nearly a month looking, and then a friend told him about a tax sale that was occurring in the county of Santa Clara, about 60 miles south of San Francisco. My dad drove there and got a list of properties that were going up for auction.

One in particular he liked was on 3 acres in a town called Los Gatos. He talked to several local brokers and learned that (even in those days) the property was worth close to $30,000. He figured that with only $3,000 he didn't have much of a chance at it.

Nevertheless he went to the auction. When the property in Los Gatos came up for bid, he didn't hesitate and immediately bid his full $3,000. I was at the sale with him

## OPPORTUNITIES IN TAX SALES

and recall his saying, "I might as well bet the whole ball of wax because as soon as the other bidders get started, I probably won't get a chance to bid at all." You can imagine his surprise when there were no other bidders. He got the property, free and clear, for the full price of $3,000! It was this investment which got him, and me, started in real estate many years ago.

### TAX SALES TODAY

"Sure," Jim said, "but you're talking ancient history. That happened back in the 1940s. I doubt that there are tax sales like that today."

Quite the contrary, I assured him. Tax sales go on today in every state and in many counties. It is possible to buy property, usually bare lots, for under $100! In some cases it is possible to buy improved property (with houses on it) for under $1,000.

"It doesn't make sense," Jim said. "Why would anyone let property like that go for what must be a lot less than its actual value?"

### REASONS WHY PROPERTY IS SOLD AT TAX SALES

There are many reasons why property ends up in tax sales today, I replied. Here are just a few:

1. *Neglect.* The former owners for whatever reason simply neglected to pay their tax bill. This is not just absentmindedness; this is active neglect. It's not because the owner isn't aware of the tax bill. Each year the owners of

# WEALTH BUILDERS

property get a tax assessment, a tax bill, and, if the bill isn't paid, a late statement. Although the procedure is different for each state, in California, for example, after failure to pay a tax bill, the property is technically sold to the state. But the owners now have *five years* in which to make up the back taxes. The property isn't auctioned off during that period of time. An owner has to be pretty determined to not pay taxes for five years. That's why I call this active neglect.

2. *Death.* In some cases the owner dies and there are no immediate heirs. The property may simply be abandoned. This is frequently the case with bare land. Neighbors to the property often have no idea who owns it or whether or not taxes have been paid. When the taxes aren't paid, the state takes it over and eventually disposes of it at auction.

3. *Lack of interest.* The owner may be aware the tax bill has come due, but he or she just isn't interested in the property anymore. Perhaps it's a lot with an old house on it that's been in the family for years. Each year this one member of the family has been paying the taxes and getting nothing in return. The house is too run-down to rent. And all the family members can't agree to sign it off so it can be sold. Finally, one year the family member who's been paying the taxes decides that he or she just isn't interested in it anymore. The taxes aren't paid, and the property slowly makes its way to the state to be sold at a tax sale.

There are many more reasons why property gets sold at tax sales, but these are the major ones.

Jim nodded. "I can see how it can happen," he said. "But why is the property sold so cheaply?"

—154—

## WHY LOW PRICES AT TAX SALES?

The prices frequently are low, I pointed out, because often the minimum bid is the amount of back taxes owed. Sometimes, however, a former owner will be there and will bid up the price to get the property back for sentimental reasons. Other times, a really valuable piece of property will be offered and the competition for it will be fierce.

But usually tax sales are in the backwash of investment. Few people even know they exist, and fewer attend the sales to bid. In fact you usually can find the same group at each sale.

Because of the lack of interest, because of the lack of competition at the bidding, because of the hassle of dealing with the government, and because of the difficulties in getting financing (remember, tax sales are *cash* sales), these auctions are lightly attended and prices are often incredibly low.

## DRAWBACKS

"It sounds too good to be true," Jim said. "The low price makes up for it all. It's all pluses. Aren't there any drawbacks?"

There are several, I pointed out. Even most of these, however, turn into advantages in the long run. The biggest is the fact that in most states the former owner has a *right of redemption* even after you buy the property. It works like this.

You attend an auction (we'll see how an auction is held and how to find out where they are in a few moments), bid on a property, and are the winner. But are you the owner?

## WEALTH BUILDERS

Yes and no. You have most owner's rights to the property. However, in most states the former owner has a set period of time in which he or she can redeem the property. Typically that time limit is one year. During that year the former owner can come back and claim the property. In that case, you *must* give up your title.

"Not good," Jim said. "Here I'm out my time and my money."

Not at all, I pointed out. The former owner doesn't simply come back and say, "Give me my property." The demand has to be backed by money. To get the property back (to exercise the right of redemption) the former owner must usually do the following:

1. Repay all of the court costs (if any) incurred when you bought the property at auction.

2. Repay in full to you the amount you paid for the property.

3. *Pay you interest* on the money you had tied up in the property from the day you bought it until the day it was redeemed. The interest rate is determined by each state, but typically it is between 12 and 18 percent.

Jim whistled. "It's hard to lose," he said. "Either I get the property, *or* I get my full money back at a high interest rate."

That's it exactly, I said. The biggest disadvantage to tax sales, the right of redemption, turns out to be one of its biggest advantages in terms of investment.

Another drawback is that the sale is all cash. That means *either* you have to come up with all the money

## OPPORTUNITIES IN TAX SALES

yourself, *or* you have to make your own arrangements for financing with a savings and loan association or bank. (This latter isn't that difficult. Just contact a lender, describe the property you're interested in, and find out what, if anything, they'll loan. The loan usually can be obtained *after* you purchase or, with a creative lender who's willing to work with you, even as part of the purchase price.)

The last drawback is the fact that *you must attend the sale.* You can't be an armchair purchaser here. You actually have to go to where the sales are and do the bidding.

Jim looked worried.

It's not hard, I said. In fact it can be a whole lot of fun. But it does take time. That's why I asked if you were willing to commit one day a month to this investment. During that day you'll have to travel to where the auction is being held and bid.

"For the prices it sounds like you can get, I'd be willing to spend a week on it!" exclaimed Jim.

A week usually isn't necessary, I said. You can write away for information on auctions and then, once a month, attend one. If you buy only one property for $100 at each auction, at the end of a year you'll own twelve properties for a total expenditure of only about $1,200!

## ARE THE PROPERTIES WORTH ANYTHING?

"That brings up an interesting point," said Jim. "I can see that occasionally there would be valuable properties offered at these sales. But chances are their prices are going to be higher than $100. What kind of a property do I get for $100? Isn't it just junk? If the former owner didn't want it, what will I do with it? Could I be buying an albatross?"

Remember, I pointed out, that you have no idea why the former owner didn't want the property. Yes, it could have been junk to him or her, or it could have been neglect, lack of interest, death, or any other reason. In today's real estate market, quite frankly, there aren't many properties which could be called junk. In today's market almost everything has a strong value.

## LOTS OF LOTS

Typically, most of the property offered at tax sales is in the form of bare land. This may be an improved lot (one with utilities, sewer, streets, and grading) or an unimproved lot. It could be in a rural or an urban setting. My guess is that for every improved parcel (one with a house on it) there are ten unimproved parcels offered at tax sales.

"But what can I do with bare land? I've heard real estate brokers say that I should stay away from it. They said you couldn't refinance it and you had trouble selling it."

Undoubtedly, they were speaking of bare land bought at full retail price, I said. Here we're talking about presumably buying far below market value. Nevertheless, it is true that land is the most difficult real estate to deal with. Typically, its selling price is much lower than improved property, and hence most brokers won't bother with it unless you offer them a 10 (or more) percent commission. And most banks and savings and loans associations won't make loans on it (because it yields no return in the form of rent). This means that unless it's in an area of rapid appreciation, buyers are hard to come by. Few people are willing to invest full price in land and then just let their money sit.

"It sounds to me like you've got a lot of reasons why

## OPPORTUNITIES IN TAX SALES

I shouldn't be interested in the lots offered at tax sales," said Jim.

### WAYS TO PROFIT ON BARE LAND BOUGHT AT A TAX SALE

I pointed out I was just trying to present a balanced picture. There are also many positive things about these lots. Here's what you can do with a lot you purchase at a tax sale.

**1. Use It for a Down Payment (Partial Trade)**
Once you own a lot, no one really knows or cares how you acquired it or how much you paid for it. Its value becomes what an appraiser says its value is. While you might have difficulty in selling it outright, for reasons we've just discussed, you might much more easily be able to use it instead of cash when making a down payment on other property.

For example, both new and existing home sellers are finding it tough to sell their homes in today's market. Frequently, high interest rates and high prices discourage buyers. In most cases they will listen to any reasonable offer. What about an offer which says that instead of 20 percent cash down, you offer a lot at a value determined by a county tax assessor?

If the seller is willing to accept it (and many sellers will, either because they see an advantage in owning a lot or because they want to get out of their present house), so too will most lenders. The lender may insist on their own appraisal of the lot, but in most cases a lot can substitute for cash in the typical 20 percent down payment required when you get a new loan on a house.

Don't think simply about real estate either. Think about other areas. Car dealers, for example, are always looking to make deals. I have seen them accept a lot as a large down payment on a car. The same holds true of anyone selling any large-ticket item.

## 2. Use It as a Charitable Donation

This is not a sure thing and you'd certainly want to check with your own tax accountant and adviser before attempting it. But some investors, *after they've owned a piece of property for one year* (the capital gains period), donate it to a legitimate charity and then deduct the current value of the property.

As I said, the tax laws and their interpretations change constantly, so you'll need to check with a good tax adviser first. But the the possibilities here are interesting. What these investors are doing is, for example, buying a lot for $100 (the amount of the back taxes owed) at a tax sale. After one year (the capital gains period) the value of the lot might be $1,000 as determined by the tax assessor of the county. Now these investors are donating the lot to a charity and taking a $1,000 deduction.

Of course, the donation might be challenged on the basis that the investor paid only $100. But then there's the county tax assessor's evaluation stating that its market value is $1,000. It makes for some interesting tax discussions.

## 3. Use It to Improve Your Financial Statement.

All of us live well or live badly as determined by our financial statement. With a good statement, bank loans, mortgages, credit cards, and other financing devices are readily available to us. With a bad statement, these can all be denied.

## OPPORTUNITIES IN TAX SALES

*Nothing improves a financial statement like paid-off real estate.* Put that lot down on your financial statement. The fact that it's paid off is going to impress any lending officer. What counts is that it is a valuable asset on which to base future lending to you.

### 4. Use It as Part of Your Vacation.

Sometimes you can buy a lot that's in a scenic area. It might be a suitable place for camping. You could travel to your lot and use it as part of a vacation.

In addition, if you own an investment lot, you normally can deduct from your taxes your business travel expenses to and from the property. If the lot happens to be near Vail or Lake Tahoe or some other scenic recreation area, it might be possible to combine a business and a pleasure trip. (However, you certainly won't be able to deduct the expenses of the recreation part of your trip.)

### 5. You Might Be Able to Build on It.

If you're selective when you bid, you should be able to obtain buildable lots. In that case you can make arrangements with a contractor to erect a house on one or more of them. (Some enterprising investors have purchased lots and then moved mobile homes on them, selling the package for a considerable profit.)

These, then, are five ways you can profit from buying a bare lot at a tax sale. But remember, it isn't only bare lots which are offered. At almost every sale there is some improved property. This is usually in the form of small, single-family homes. But there have been sales where duplexes, small commercial buildings, and even an apartment building were offered! (Of course, the bidding was fast and furious for these. Nevertheless, these large items still tend to sell for substantially less than market value.)

"You've convinced me," said Jim. "How do I do it?"

## FINDING OUT ABOUT TAX SALES

The first thing you need to do, I pointed out, is to determine where and when tax sales are going to be held. That's not as hard as it seems. While it's not practical to give a list here for whom to contact in every county or township nationwide, the procedure is the same regardless of where you live. To find out about tax sales near you, just write or call the county official who handles tax sales. The title of this official varies regionally, but here are typical titles:

1. County treasurer
2. County auditor
3. County tax collector
4. County sheriff
5. County trustee
6. Clerk of the county court

Once you've contacted this person's office, they will send you a public notice for the next tax sale. The notice will outline in detail where, when, and under what conditions the auction will be held.

## LIST OF PROPERTIES TO BE OFFERED

In addition to the sale notice you will also receive a list of the properties offered, briefly describing them and giving their location.

# OPPORTUNITIES IN TAX SALES

"I use the list to inspect the properties, right?" Jim asked.

I could see he was the sort who wanted to act immediately once he became enthused about a project. I wanted to encourage him, but not send him off half-cocked.

Indeed you should spend one day examining the properties, I pointed out. However, frequently there are dozens offered and it might be wasted energy trying to track them all down. A method of conserving energy that some investors use is to simply bid on properties that others are bidding on, following the theory that these properties are the best deal.

## TRAVELING TO THE SALE

"But are sales held every month in every county?" asked Jim.

No, I pointed out, they are held only occasionally as needed. That means that you might have to travel to counties across the state or even out-of-state to be able to attend a sale every month.

## PREPARING FOR THE SALE

"Then I just go there and bid, right?" Jim asked.

His enthusiasm was still high. That is almost right, I pointed out. However, you will have to check the public notices to see what form the bidding will be in. Typically, you will need to have a cashier's check for a minimum amount of money.

Also, before attending the sale you'll want to check with a title insurance company in the area to be certain that you could get clear title. (At a tax sale, property is offered "as is" and without any kind of warranty by the state. You want to be sure that there isn't any problem with the title and that in your area a tax sale deed is, in fact, a good clear title to the property. Sometimes there are claims to property from previous lenders or owners. Usually, *but not always*, these are cleared by the tax sale deed.)

Once you've examined the properties, you should make a list of those on which you want to bid. Now you should determine how much you're willing to bid. (As I mentioned, typically the minimum bid, if any, is the amount of back taxes.) A good rule to follow is to make sure that your bid for the property is never more than one-seventh of the assessed valuation. In this way you have a fairly safe way of knowing that you won't be paying more than you should for a property. You can determine an approximation of its real value by getting the assessed valuation from the county assessor.

## ATTENDING THE SALE

Attending a tax sale is one of the great experiences of the world. It is a combination of American free enterprise and a Turkish bazaar. Emotions can run high, and some bidders are not above trying psychological warfare to get you out of the bidding.

One common approach is for experienced bidders to come up to you the minute you walk into the room and attempt to gain your confidence. They will appear friendly, ask if it's your first time, and offer to help you get qualified. ("Getting qualified" simply means going to the person handling the sale, showing that you have a cashier's check for the appropriate amount, and registering your name.)

These experienced bidders are trying to find out the following:

## OPPORTUNITIES
## IN TAX SALES

   1. Are you a former owner of a piece of property bidding for sentimental reasons? If so, which property? They probably won't bid against you because they know you'll go too high. (See the section below on "den of thieves.")
   2 Are you a speculator like them? If so, they may try to direct you away from the "hot" properties that they want to bid on.
   3. What's your perception of "price"? If you appear to have a lot of money and are unsure of how much to pay, they may match your bidding at first so that you pay too much for one or two properties, hoping you'll get discouraged and drop out.

   "Sounds like I could get in over my head." Jim looked worried.

   I smiled. Everyone has a first time. Just be friendly, don't reveal too much, and at the same time, try to find out from these experienced investors exactly what they're trying to find out from you. Once you catch on that it's a game, it can be quite amusing and entertaining.

   Once the bidding starts, if possible, wait until at least a third of the way through the properties before bidding. Typically the highest prices come right at the beginning and again right at the end. At the beginning, the bidders have lots of money and frequently go too high. At the end, they realize these are the last properties and bid up the price lest they miss out.

   Make your bids. Don't be hesitant. It's a free country, and each bidder has an equal opportunity.

   Keep your bids small the first time out. It's not the end of the world if you overbid and pay more than you wanted to in the heat of the contest if you still end up paying only $100 for a property! Until you're more experienced, avoid the higher-priced real estate.

## WATCH OUT FOR THE "DEN OF THIEVES"

"It sounds better than poker night or a day at a carnival!" Jim's enthusiasm had returned.

I said that I believed some investors went there not so much for the profits possible, but just for the thrill of bidding. However, it was important to watch out for the "den of thieves."

Jim looked puzzled, so I explained. I said it is indeed like poker. In an honest poker game, each player is independent, but in a rigged game, often two or three players work together to soak the others. The same sometimes happens at these sales.

Sometimes a group of investors will band together in what I call a "den of thieves." They will attend a sale and agree among themselves which properties they want. Then they will force the bidding up on other properties and hold it back on these. The result is that they get their properties for a lower price.

If they find you are bidding against them, they may quickly force the bidding up over your limit and squeeze you out. After they've done this once or twice, you'll recognize what's happening and then won't bid against them. At that point, they'll reduce their bidding and try again to get the properties at an artificially cheap price.

"How do I fight that?" Jim was beginning to falter again.

Don't worry. They often don't show up at sales. And if they do, a bidder who's independent such as you, frequently can outsmart them. Just continue to bid what you think you should on properties. When they see you're determined and that you'll stop at a certain price, they'll come

## OPPORTUNITIES IN TAX SALES

to realize that either they'll have to overbid you and pay more than they want for properties, or they'll have to let you have a few.

Where they are really effective and terrible is with someone such as a former owner who wants the house at any price. Once they zero in on such a person, they'll continue to bid with him forcing the price up ridiculously high. At this point they've been known to approach the now distraught sentimental buyer and agree to stop bidding if he or she will pay each of them a hundred dollars or so. More than one sentimental buyer has agreed and they've made a "profit" with no expenditure at all.

"But, isn't that illegal?" asked Jim.

It might be, I said, but it nevertheless can happen. Every investment has a darker side, and this happens to be it for tax sales.

### THE BOTTOM LINE

It's important to understand that you can do well at tax sales in any economic climate. It makes no difference whether interest rates are high or low (unless you're arranging financing) or inflation is high or low. These sales go on year in and year out, and the prices are always low.

"I'm going to get started."

Great, I said. Only don't forget to write down your plan. In the short run, write down which properties you'll bid on and the maximum you'll pay and don't pay more. In the long run determine what you're going to do with the properties you acquire at tax sales *before* you acquire them.

## THE PENNY STOCK BOOM

**RISK**
High

**WHEN TO BUY**
Inflation—low
Interest rates—moderate

**WHEN TO SELL**
Inflation—low
Interest rates—moderate

**HOLDING PERIOD**
Usually short

**MINIMUM CASH REQUIRED**
$1,000

**PROFIT POTENTIAL**
High

**SKILL REQUIRED**
Moderate (good understanding
of field is necessary)

**EFFORT REQUIRED**
May be done as a hobby

**MAJOR DIFFICULTY**
Finding good new issues

# CHAPTER NINE
# THE PENNY STOCK BOOM

Gail had been a member of the Future Millionaires' Investment Club since its inception. She said she believed in strictly conservative investments—T-bills, insured money market accounts, certificates of deposit. Consequently I was surprised when the first thing she asked about was penny stocks.

Penny stocks can only be considered a high-risk investment, I explained. The profit potential is enormous, but risk is limited. You can't lose more than you invest. (You can in the commodity futures market.) I said that her interest seemed uncharacteristic.

"I'm tired of watching everybody else get rich," she explained. "I could sit around with my money in 'safe' investments for the rest of my life. I've decided I want to take a plunge. Not with everything I own, of course. I've taken $1,500—10 percent of my capital—and I've decided that I want to play the risk game with it. If I win, I'll reinvest. If I lose, I'll wait till I build up my capital and try again."

In other words, I clarified, you're playing with money you feel you can afford to lose.

"I don't want to lose it," she explained. "But if I do, well then it's not the end of the world."

Because she had only $1,500 to invest, she had decided on penny stocks. "I really don't have enough for a plunge in the regular stock market. But I think I can be a big buyer in penny stocks."

I nodded that $1,500 was certainly enough for a plunge.

## WHAT ARE PENNY STOCKS?

I pointed out that penny stocks are really any stock that sells for a low price. In the industry, any stock selling for under $5 is usually called a penny stock. Most penny stocks, however, sell for a dollar a share or less. There are some that do indeed sell for a cent a share.

"That's what I've heard," Gail said. "But I still wonder if any of those stocks are good? After all I've always believed that you get what you pay for. If you're buying something cheap, it usually means there's a good reason the price is low. Could it be that they're called 'pennies' because they aren't worth anything?"

## DO PENNY STOCKS HAVE REAL VALUE?

Indeed, I pointed out, often the reason a stock is selling for a very low price is because it really isn't worth anything. But that isn't always the case. To understand why, you have to understand why penny stocks even exist.

When a company such as General Motors or Xerox or IBM or any of the industrial giants decides to issue new stock, it typically prices that stock at a figure that will insure its quick sale, yet will bring in a lot of revenue. Rarely will such stock be issued for under $10 a share.

Investors are willing to pay a higher price for shares

# THE PENNY STOCK BOOM

of stock in such companies because they know the company has:

1. Enormous assets
2. Strong potential earnings
3. An impressive track record
4. Capable management (to move the company forward)
5. A substantial market share for its products

In fact assets, earnings, track record, management, and market share help make GM, Xerox, and IBM the giants that they are.

## A TYPICAL PENNY STOCK COMPANY

Now consider a different kind of company. This is a company that has only four owners, Mac, Imogene, Norman, and Timothy. They are all experts in genetic engineering (Timothy also has a little background in management and finance). They call their company MINT (after the first letters of their names).

For the past three years the owners of MINT have been struggling to perfect a drug that will be a "magic bullet" for cancer. It will enter the blood stream of a patient and kill only cancer cells.

"That would be a miracle," said Gail.

It certainly would, I replied. And the company that owned the patent to that drug would be worth millions, perhaps billions, of dollars. Now after three years of experimenting, MINT thinks it's on the right track. But to develop and test its drug, it needs several millions of dollars. How is it going to raise that money?

## PROBLEMS RAISING CAPITAL

"It could get a bank loan or the owners could go to a major pharmaceutical house," replied Gail.

Both are good ideas, I replied. However, banks (and other lenders) don't lend on the basis of "maybe" profits in the future. They lend on collateral. Between them, the owners of MINT couldn't raise more than $150,000 in collateral, most of that in their home equities.

On the other hand, if they go to a major pharmaceutical house, they most certainly will have to give up both control of their project and, more importantly, the lion's share of their profits. Remember, these are staunchly independent people. They've each committed three years of their lives with little or no pay to develop this product. They're not about to give up future profits without a fight.

"I guess they're stuck when it comes to raising money," said Gail.

## ENTERING THE VENTURE-CAPITAL MARKET

They're between that old rock and a hard place, I replied. They can't borrow the funds and they don't want to give up the profits. An alternative is the venture-capital market. This is a market where speculators are willing to bet on small companies such as these.

But there are problems even here. If they approach a major speculator who is willing to give them the required funds, you can be sure that speculator is going to want at least 90 percent control of their company. And that speculator is going to be hounding them day and night for results, always threatening to cut off funds and back out. It

# THE PENNY STOCK BOOM

would be like taking in a partner who happened to be Attila the Hun.

"So there really are no solutions, then?" Gail asked.

The last, best alternative for MINT is the stock market. Instead of taking in a single venture-capital partner, the owners of MINT decide to issue stock. They'll offer $2 million worth of shares to the general public. In this fashion they hope to raise the capital they need, have thousands of small, anonymous shareholders (instead of a single large partner), and still retain full control of the company (by issuing to themselves more shares than they sell to the public).

## PROBLEMS WITH A SMALL COMPANY GOING PUBLIC

"Sounds like a great idea," said Gail.

It is, except for one drawback, I replied. Who will buy stock in a company that has:

1. No assets?
2. No potential earnings?
3. No track record?
4. No experience in managing this type of company?
5. No market share for its products?

Remember, these five items were what allowed the major companies to sell stock. MINT has none of these.

"I can see it's a problem. I wouldn't pay $10 a share for stock in that company."

Neither would anybody else with any common sense, I agreed. But would you be willing to pay 25 cents a share? If you knew the background in genetic engineering of the

MINT developers, if you knew they were on the road to a possible cancer cure, if you knew they were going to use *all* of the money raised to try to develop and produce this miracle drug, would you risk 25 cents a share (or the required $250 for a "block" of 1,000 shares) on the company?

Gail thought for a moment. "It's a real gamble, isn't it?" I nodded. "Yes, I would," she finally replied. "I'm looking for a long shot and this seems like it. If they don't succeed, well then I'm out my $250. But if they make it, that stock could soon be worth $10 a share or a lot more. My $250 investment could eventually turn into $10,000 or who knows how much more! Yes, I really would!"

Then you understand the penny stock market, I explained. It's highly speculative. You're betting on unproven companies, hoping that they will beat the odds against them and succeed. Usually you're buying either new stock like MINT's as it's issued (called *new issues* or the primary market) or the stock of an existing small company which you feel may be on the brink of a big spurt in value (usually called the *aftermarket* or secondary market). You put up your money and you take your chance.

"But look at the profits I could make. I could make a dollar back for every penny I invest!"

Yes, I replied, and there are many success stories, IBM and Xerox among them. But for every penny stock company that succeeds, there are more that fail. (That's one reason I always recommend spreading your money around several companies—so your chance of hitting a winner may be improved.)

"I'm not worried. How do I get started?" Gail asked.

It's not complicated, I explained, but there are a number of things you have to know and we'll discuss these shortly. But first, you have to be sure you understand the basic conditions of the market.

## BASIC CONDITIONS OF PENNY STOCK INVESTMENT

1. *It's high risk.* You can easily lose all your money.
2. The risk is not only in the companies themselves, but in the market, which can be highly volatile (we'll discuss this shortly).
3. There are some important government restrictions which may affect your ability to invest.
4. This is an area were there are "suede shoe" salesmen—promoters and crooks ready to take advantage of the unwary.

If you understand the basic conditions of the market and accept them, then you're ready to begin with your investing, I said. Gail nodded. She was still enthusiastic.

The two areas in which you can invest are either in new issues or in aftermarket stocks (stocks previously issued), I explained. We'll consider each separately, but first let's get a handle on what the penny stock market really is.

## THE PENNY STOCK MARKET

Where do you suppose you buy penny stocks? I asked Gail. She replied, "From my stockbroker, I assume. I just call him up and tell him I want to buy."

It's a natural assumption, I said. However, it's not usually the case that your average stockbroker will be able to handle all your penny stock transactions. For example, though your broker may be able to handle most aftermarket purchases for you, it is most unlikely he or she could get you in on the ground floor of a new issue. Gail looked puzzled.

I said I'd explain that when we talked about new issues. But first, I wanted to explain about the two "different kinds" of stock markets that exist. On the one hand there is the typical stockbroker, who deals primarily with stocks listed on the Big Board (the New York Stock Exchange), the American Stock Exchange, and *major* over-the-counter markets.

Then, on the other hand, there is the specialist penny stockbroker who deals almost exclusively with the less common over-the-counter market—with individual brokers and market makers. (We'll get to the term "market maker" in a moment.)

## THE OVER-THE-COUNTER (OTC) MARKET

"I've never heard of two different stock markets," said Gail. "I thought there was only one market, the New York Stock Exchange. And what does 'over the counter' mean?"

I pointed out that most people new to stocks indeed consider only the New York Stock Exchange. Most of the country's big stocks are indeed listed on the Big Board (the New York Stock Exchange) or the American Stock Exchange. However, to be listed in these two markets, most stocks usually have to sell for $5 a share or more. If a stock

# THE PENNY STOCK BOOM

drops below $5 for any extended period of time, it can be delisted. (Actually the major stock exchanges have specific guidelines for listing and delisting a stock, and the stock price is not usually a major factor. However, it is a fact that when a company's attributes are dropping below the guidelines, the stock value is often also dropping below $5.) These markets are for the established stocks, for the IBMs and the General Motors. But remember, we're dealing with a tiny company like MINT. There's no place for it on either the Big Board or the American Exchange.

"That makes sense," agreed Gail. "But then where is it listed?"

Actually, I replied, the penny stocks aren't really listed on an exchange anywhere in this country. (In Canada, on the other hand, the Vancouver Exchange is a real penny stock market exchange.) Rather, they are handled by individual stockbrokers acting as market makers. Perhaps this can best be seen if we continue with our example of MINT.

## MINT'S STOCK ISSUE

MINT has decided to issue stock to the public. To do this it must get Securities and Exchange Commission approval, which it does. (We'll have more to say about this later.) Now, how does it go about selling the stock it is going to issue?

During the sales period, MINT can sell the stock itself from its corporate offices. However, for better marketing it will probably choose to find a well-known stockbroker who has the best reputation possible for bringing out new stocks, to promote the sale for it. MINT makes the following arrangements with such a stockbroker. In exchange for MINT's paying the broker's expenses in the sale, the broker will agree to underwrite the stock and make a market for it after the sale.

## THE MARKET MAKER

Here are two important concepts. The *underwriter* is the stockbrokerage company which agrees to promote the sale of MINT's new issue. The *market maker* is the stockbrokerage house which agrees that *after* the new issues are sold (the aftermarket), it will continue to buy and sell the MINT stock—in other words to carry an inventory of the stock (maintain liquidity in the market). Normally the underwriter will also be the market maker.

Gail looked puzzled. "I think I know what you mean by 'underwriter'—that's a broker who sells the new stock that MINT is issuing." I nodded. "But I'm not sure why there has to be a market maker?"

Think of it this way, I explained. MINT sells several million shares of new stock. Now some owners of this stock want to sell it. New investors, on the other hand, want to buy it. Who handles the transactions for them?

One alternative would be for MINT itself to handle these transactions. But, if there are going to be many transactions, it's better if a brokerage firm with experience in stocks handles them. Consequently, MINT will find a broker who will keep an inventory of MINT stocks always ready to sell to any investor who wants to buy. And the same broker will always be ready to buy from any investor who wants to sell. This broker makes a market, or creates liquidity, in MINT stocks—he's a market maker. Gail nodded.

MINT looks for the biggest broker they can find who

## THE PENNY STOCK BOOM

will agree to handle their new-issue stock and comes up with Stanley and Lester Evans Securities (SALES). SALES will handle MINT's stock.

During the sales period for MINT's new issue, SALES will offer the stock to the public and get as many as possible of its own clients to buy it. Once the stock is fully subscribed (sold out) and issued, SALES will become the market maker and will agree to buy stock from anyone who wants to sell and sell stock to anyone who wants to buy. SALES is now doing just what its title says: it's selling as an underwriter and it's buying and selling as a market maker.

### BUYING A PENNY STOCK

"That's all very interesting," said Gail. "But what does it have to do with my purchasing a penny stock?"

I'm just coming to that, I said. Let's say that you've heard about MINT and want to buy its stocks. It's too late to get a new issue, but you can buy in the aftermarket. You go to your broker and say you want to buy some shares. Your broker shakes her head. She's never heard about MINT, but she can find out. Your broker now goes to her computer, where thousands of stocks are listed. She doesn't call up the Big Board or the American, but instead she calls up NASDAQ (the National Association of Securities Dealers Automated Quotations)—the largest computerized system for the kinds of stocks we're discussing. If it were a major offering nationwide, MINT would be listed here. However, MINT is a small offering and it's not on the national computer.

Now your broker calls a broker in a city nearby, where MINT is located, and asks if they've heard of the stock. This broker checks to find out who the local market maker is and finds MINT listed. He tells your broker that the market maker is SALES.

Your broker now calls up SALES (the market maker maintaining liquidity in MINT stocks) and says she wants to buy a thousand shares (1,000 is usually the smallest block sold of penny stocks). SALES checks and says that MINT is currently *bid* at 20 cents, *ask* at 25 cents.

"You've lost me," said Gail. "I only wanted to buy the stock. What is this business with bid and ask?

## BID AND ASK

Remember, I said, that SALES is making a market on MINT stock. But it isn't doing this for free. It is doing it to make a profit. In addition, it has expenses, such as the cost of keeping an inventory of MINT stock. And it has risks; what if MINT stock should suddenly fall in value while SALES is maintaining an inventory?

Therefore, to cover its expenses and profit, SALES maintains a *spread* on the price of the stock. It will buy the stock from anyone who wants to sell at 20 cents (this is the *bid* price). It will sell the stock to anyone who wants to buy for 25 cents. This is the ask price. The 5 cents between the bid and ask is the spread. (The more liquid the stock—more transactions—and the higher the price, usually the lower the spread. The less liquid the stock and the lower the price, the higher the spread.)

Your broker now turns to you and says that you have to pay 25 cents a share to buy MINT. That's $250. You agree. Your broker now concludes the sale with the SALES broker. You pay your money, and within a matter of weeks you'll get your stock. (In actual practice there is usually an area of each stock office reserved for these phone transactions and a special broker who handles them and who tries to get the best price for you.)

## THE OTC MARKET

This process of dickering for price and handling it between brokers without the clearinghouse process of an exchange is called an over-the-counter market. You can find the major OTC stocks listed by NASDAQ through their computer service in most major newspapers and certainly in the *Wall Street Journal*. You can learn about smaller markets only through individual brokers.

"It certainly is complicated," said Gail.

Not really, I replied. It may sound complex when you first hear it. But it really works quite smoothly. In our example, MINT had only one market maker, which made finding out about the stock rather difficult. However, a larger company will often have many brokerage houses acting as market makers all around the country, so that locating their stock becomes quite easy. Also, there are thousands and thousands of stocks listed by computer. In most cases a computer check will turn up the stock you're looking for.

"I'm pretty sure I understand," said Gail. "But let's get to the important stuff. How do I make a profit once I buy?"

## PROFITING FROM THE AFTERMARKET

In our example, I pointed out, you bought stock in the aftermarket. In other words, the stock wasn't newly issued. Rather you were buying indirectly probably from another investor who was selling.

# WEALTH BUILDERS

You now have to wait. Your profits will come when you sell if MINT's stock soars in value because:

1. MINT perfects its drug and either markets or sells its patent.
2. MINT begins earning profits (either on the original drug or because of some other developments).
3. Speculators believe MINT is going to do well, and they bid up the stock's price.
4. Something unexpected happens to boost MINT's stock value.

In other words, I explained, you must now play a waiting game. It's just the same as if you bought IBM or Chrysler. You have to wait until the company's fortunes turn up for the stock to turn up in value. Then you sell.

"But, how's that different from buying a major stock?" asked Gail. "It sounds the same."

## HOW HOLDING PENNY STOCKS DIFFERS FROM HOLDING MAJOR STOCKS

In theory it is the same, I explained. However, in practice it's a bit different. If a large investor buys GM, for example, and the stock goes up by 25 percent in value, the investor's probably going to be very pleased. Chances are this large investor has bought 10,000 shares, and if the stock moved from $60 to $75 a share that's a total increase of $150,000.

## THE PENNY STOCK BOOM

On the other hand, let's say MINT is worth only a dollar a share. An increase of 25 percent takes it to $1.25. (An investor who owns 10,000 shares now gets an increase of $2,500.) However, with the success of a new drug it could jump to $50 a share in value (a fiftyfold increase), and the investor would make $500,000.

In other words, with a tiny company the chance of a big increase in value from a new discovery is far more likely than for a huge company. (An active day's trading of MINT's stock with no big discovery could push it up 25 cents a share—a 25 percent increase. It would be almost impossible for simple active trading to boost GM $15 a share (given the prices in our example).

It's also far easier in terms of its product line. MINT needs only one drug to, for example, make $100 million and get a fiftyfold increase in stock value. If GM had the same drug and made the same $100 million, its stock value might increase only perhaps 2 or 3 percent.

"I think I see what you mean," said Gail. "With a small company it's far easier to get a large percentage increase in value than with a large one."

Correct, I said. Unfortunately, it also goes the other way. It's also far easier for such a company to go bankrupt. It simply doesn't have the assets to hold it through a rough period.

### WHICH PENNY STOCK TO BUY IN THE AFTERMARKET

"So what you're saying, then," said Gail, "is that I buy any cheap penny stock and hold it until it jumps in value."

Not at all, I pointed out. Most penny stock won't jump

## WEALTH BUILDERS

in value. Statistics indicate that most companies will not succeed, but rather will fail. You will make profit by selecting just the right company.

"How do I know which company is right?"

That, I said, takes some research and some luck. In general those penny stocks which have done well over the past few years have fallen into three groups.*

### Group 1—Mining Stocks

These are stocks mostly from gold and silver mining companies and oil drilling.

Most people are familiar with gold mining companies such as Homestake, but the penny stock companies which have shown real volatility have been the small mining companies around Denver and in Canada. In fact, the Vancouver Stock Exchange, which trades as many as forty million penny stock shares a day, comprises mostly mining companies. The key here is usually the price of the precious metal. As metal prices have soared, so have the penny stock shares of many mining companies. As metal prices have fallen, so have the stocks.

With oil exploration companies, it's the success or failure of wells that counts. One company, Ross Exploration, struck oil in not one, but six wells in Pennsylvania in 1983. Its stock went from 10 cents a share to over $1 a share by 1984.

### Group 2—High-Tech Stocks

These are companies in various high-tech fields. Generally, computers and health stocks have been winners in the

---

* The success, or lack of it, of companies mentioned here refers to their status at the time of this writing. Their fortunes could have changed dramatically in either direction since then.

—184—

## THE PENNY STOCK BOOM

past, although both have been soft lately. Techniclone opened trading in January of 1983 at 1 cent a share. By late in the year it was up to nearly 9 cents a share (a 900 percent increase).

Those companies which provide high-tech solutions to modern problems have been the ones which have done particularly well in the past. (A company such as our mythical MINT would fit in here.) Robotics (such as Fared Robot and Robot Defense Systems) have been a hot area of this group.

### Group 3—Promotional Companies

This group involves companies which promote products. A good example here would probably be Twistee Freeze. It came out with a program for opening small specialty ice cream stores in shopping-center parking lots and initially did very well.

### FINDING OUT ABOUT PENNY STOCKS

"But I've never heard of any of these stocks," said Gail. "Would my broker know about them?"

Probably not, I replied, unless your broker specialized in pennies. As I mentioned, because of greater visibility, most brokers find it more profitable to work the Big Board.

"All right, you've convinced me. How do I find a penny stockbroker?"

I could give you a list of names of penny stockbrokers, I replied. However, that might quickly get outdated. I have a better answer to your question. There are a number of publications that serve the penny stock market field. I'm going to suggest three. They each list major brokers and frequently give addresses and/or phone numbers. But in addition, they can also each give you valuable current information on the penny stocks. They are:

*Low-Priced Stock Digest* and *Penny Stock Preview* (Monthly newsletters). Both are published by Idea Publishing Corporation, 55 East Afton Avenue, Yardley, PA 19067. Recent price for the *Digest* was $68 a year, for the *Preview*, $35 a year.

*Penny Stock News* (weekly newspaper) 8930 Oakland Center, Route 108, Columbia, MD 21045.

You can get a sample copy either for free or for a minimal charge by writing to these companies.

## WHEN TO BUY

"So I get these publications, read about penny stocks, find a broker, and buy. It's that simple?" asked Gail.

There's a little bit more, I replied. These publications and brokers can get you aimed in the right direction. But there are other factors you ought to consider. As I've mentioned to other members of the club, outside factors, principally inflation and interest rates affect investments. That's the case here, too.

There's an old rule about penny stocks. It goes that they are "the first and the last to run." When the stock market is just beginning to take off and just before it peters

## THE PENNY STOCK BOOM

out is when penny stocks tend to do their best as a group. Consequently, one area to watch is the overall stock market. If it's in the doldrums, chances are penny stocks will be the same way. But if the market is just beginning to show signs of rebirth or if we're at the end of a market expansion, check out the pennies. They may be leading the way.

In addition there are overall trends. Quite frankly, during the early 1980s stocks have been at their lowest ratio of earnings-to-price in decades. Many analysts are pointing to the mid- and late 1980s as the era of stocks. If they are correct, then those who buy good companies early will make the biggest profits at the end of the decade. (Of course, high inflation and high interest rates triggered by huge government deficits could upset this applecart.)

### NEW ISSUES

"You mentioned something about new issues before. What are the opportunities there?" asked Gail.

New issues, I replied, are the cream of the penny stocks. When you handle them correctly, they are your fastest vehicle to profits. Sometimes you can double or triple your investment in weeks. (Of course, it works the other way around as well. You could lose your investment in weeks, too.)

Relatively few people had heard about penny stocks until news of huge profits in new issues surfaced in the early 1980s. Since then, new issues have taken the headlines. Everyone who gets involved in penny stocks very quickly gravitates to this area. However, I've held off mentioning it until now because it's important that you have a basic understanding of the penny stock market before you broach the subject.

"I understand what new issues are. They are new stock issued by a company," said Gail. "MINT went public and issued stock. They were a new issue. What I don't understand is how do you make money on them?"

## PROFITS FROM NEW ISSUES

Big profits from new issues, when we get down to basics, come from speculation. Some investors speculate that newly issued stock will be worth more in the aftermarket than it was selling for at the new-issue price. They buy as many of the new issues as possible, then when the issue is sold out and trading begins in the aftermarket and with success the price jumps up, they sell for a profit.

"I don't get it," said Gail. "Why should prices jump in the aftermarket?"

Let's go back to our hypothetical company, MINT. We'll say that MINT is issuing 8 million shares at 25 cents a share. MINT has issued a prospectus which describes the company. It tells about what they'll do with the money, who the principal stockholders and owners are, what the field is, and what its chances for success are.

Investors reading this prospectus are really impressed. Many of them are convinced that MINT is really onto something, that it will indeed come up with a cancer cure. They want the stock so they can get in on the ground floor.

Enthusiasm for MINT stock builds. SALES, the underwriter, has no trouble selling the stock. In fact, it sells out long before the closing date. (MINT has only about three months in which to sell a minimum set percentage

# THE PENNY STOCK BOOM

of its stock or it will have to cancel the issue.) Yet, there are still many investors clamoring for MINT's stock. These investors who got left out in the cold tell their brokers to buy as soon as the stock opens in the aftermarket.

The day the aftermarket opens there are all these buy orders. Given the law of supply and demand, when there is great demand and a limited supply, the price goes up. MINT stock jumps the first day to 50 cents a share. By the end of the week it's at $1.25.

Among all those investors who are betting on MINT's long-term success, there are some speculators who couldn't care less about MINT. They simply bought a new issue hoping that things would turn out exactly as they did. Now they sell. If they bought a thousand shares at 25 cents and they sell at a dollar, they've made a 400 percent profit. And that's in a matter of weeks!

## TOO MANY SPECULATORS

"That sounds great!" said Gail. "All I have to do is get into a new issue and then sell."

The whole thing works, I said, as long as we have a stock from a company that really is a good investment and as long as we have lots of investors buying that stock to hold.

A problem can arise, however, when there are too many speculators. People such as you and I begin to see what's happening in the marketplace. We say to ourselves, "Why should I buy and hold when I can buy the new issue and then quickly turn around and sell it as soon as the aftermarket opens?"

The result is that instead of getting *long-term* investors to buy the stock, in some cases the underwriter ends up with a bunch of speculators. The stock quickly sells out, but then when it opens in the aftermarket, the speculators all try to sell at once to get their quick profit. Unless it's an unbelievably good company, there are far more speculators than long-term investors. There's a bigger supply of stock than demand and the price plummets. Instead of jumping up fourfold, the price could fall to a quarter of the new issue value, all within a week.

"Does that happen often?" wondered Gail.

Often, I replied, when the penny stock market gets overheated.

## WHY IT'S HARD TO GET NEW ISSUES

"How do I avoid getting into one of these overspeculated new issues?" asked Gail.

There are a few things you can do, I replied. But you should make it your business to know the integrity of the underwriter. (Sometimes the quality of the underwriter is more important than the quality of the stock!)

If the underwriter has integrity, it can work hard and make every effort to see that mostly long-term investors buy the new-issue stock. This is to the underwriter's advantage, assuming the same firm will later be the market maker. It costs the market maker money if the stock plunges in value right after issue (remember, the market maker is carrying some stock in his inventory—which also loses value in a plunge).

This is why every investor who tries to get new-issue stock *always* says he or she is going to hold long-term and

## THE PENNY STOCK BOOM

*never* admits they are going to sell quickly in the aftermarket. A brokerage house that is sufficiently large to handle the new issue and which has good integrity, however, will look more closely at an investor's track record than his or her promises. If you've bought and held in the past, the broker won't be hesitant to sell to you now. If you've bought and quickly sold in the past, however, a careful broker might think twice about offering you a new issue.

"Can a broker do that?" asked Gail. "Can a broker refuse to sell me stock?"

As a practical matter, yes. The broker can say the issue is oversubscribed. If more people want to buy than there is stock available, the broker picks and chooses whom he wants to sell to. As a result, sometimes it can be very hard to get new issues, particularly the good ones from the good brokers.

"How do I get them, then?" asked Gail.

I replied that I had found three techniques were useful:

**1.** Identify the reputable brokers and establish a working relationship with several of them. Buy and sell stock through them occasionally so they come to know and trust you.

**2.** Be sure your brokers regularly come out with new issues and that they know that you are very interested and want to buy them. When you get a new issue, don't immediately dump it in the aftermarket. This gives problems to your broker. Try to hold it a while if possible. Your broker will remember.

**3.** Buy only hard-to-get new issues. Stay away from a new issue when your broker tells you he can "get you all you want."

## THE PROSPECTUS—THE
## CRITERION FOR NEW ISSUES

"I don't get it," said Gail. "It sounds like I just have a standing order for new issues. As soon as one comes out, I grab it. Don't I have to analyze the stock?"

Certainly you do, I replied. We've only been talking about finding a way for you to have the opportunity to buy. Once you have that opportunity, you must decide whether or not the company warrants investing your money.

You will want to get a copy of the prospectus and read it thoroughly before you invest. However, remember that we're not dealing with GM or Xerox. We're dealing with companies like MINT. Many of the old criteria for judging stock values such as assets, earnings, and market share don't really hold up with a start-up company.

(The prospectus is what the Securities and Exchange Commission [SEC] requires of each company before it can issue stock. The SEC checks the prospectus for accuracy, but does not make a value judgment on it. Just because a company issues a prospectus *does not mean that it has been judged a safe investment*. It just means that the information in the prospectus *probably* is accurate.)

## FOUR THINGS TO WATCH OUT
## FOR IN THE PROSPECTUS

Reading a prospectus can be a science in itself, I observed. Frequently they are dozens of pages of tiny type. However, there are four things that I pay particular attention to:

1. *What is the company going to do with the money it raises?* If it's going to spend it all on product development, that's a plus. If it's going to spend most of it on officers' salaries, that's a minus.

## THE PENNY STOCK BOOM

2. *What is the management experience of the officers?* Bad management sinks more companies than any other factor. A company may have a great idea and a great product, but bad management can quickly sink it with labor problems, troubles with suppliers, and inefficient money handling.

3. *What is the company's product and does it fill a need?* This is a judgment each investor has to make. Basically what you're asking is whether or not the company has something worthwhile to offer the public. Some companies do and some don't.

4. *Are there any lawsuits pending against the company?* You might want to reconsider a company which is about to enter litigation.

Of course, there are other areas you want to check, such as the background of the officers, who is going to retain control, what is the dilution, and more.

(Here's how dilution works. If the company offers 1 million shares to the public for $1 million, yet the officers retain a second million shares for themselves and there are no assets other than the money raised from the stock sale, then the stock is diluted 50 percent. [A total of $1 million is raised, yet there are 2 million shares—$1 million/2 million shares = 50 percent. Each share for which you paid $1, is worth 50 cents in terms of assets.] Of course, there's more than assets at stake. There are also future earnings. So the dilution may not be noticed in the aftermarket.)

### PROMOTERS—THE OTHER BIG PROBLEM WITH NEW ISSUES

"So I have to get a good broker and read the prospectus, right?" asked Gail.

Right, I said. *You particularly want to pay attention to that prospectus in a hot market.* The reason is that when the penny market heats up, as it occasionally does, everyone and his uncle wants to get new issues. There simply aren't enough good companies to go around.

At this time the "suede shoe" salesmen appear. These are the same people who sell phony diamonds and discount gold. Seeing the enormous demand for new issues, they create them out of thin air. I have seen companies offering stock where there was no product, where the money raised from the stock was to go entirely as bonuses to the officers, where there was almost no chance of making money at any time in the future, and *where all these facts were clearly stated in the prospectus!* Yet the company still sold stock because the market was so hot that newcomers jumped in for anything that was available.

## OTHER ITEMS TO LOOK OUT FOR—WARRANTS AND UNITS

Sometimes instead of a stock we can buy a warrant. A warrant gives you the right (but does not obligate you) to buy a stock at a future date for a fixed price. It's very much like an option (discussed in Chapter Seven).

Sometimes, if we think a company is going to do very well but we don't want to put up the entire value of the stock, we may be able to obtain a warrant. We only invest a part of the stock's cost. If the stock goes up, as we anticipate, we can then buy at the lower fixed price of the warrant and resell the stock for a profit. Or we can simply sell our warrant.

The price of the warrant is determined by what the fixed value of it is in relation to the market and the time until it expires. (A warrant allowing us to purchase a stock for $1.50 in one week when today's price of that stock is only $1.00, is probably worthless. On the other hand, a warrant that allows us to purchase a stock for $1.00 in three months when today's price is already $1.50, is undoubtedly worth a great deal.)

Warrants are used to increase leverage in stock purchases. Because they cost only a fraction of the price of stock, for the same investment you can buy many more warrants than stocks. If the stock does well, the warrant can earn you a splendid return.

But warrants can also be bad news. They are sometimes a pesky problem when they are associated with new issues. Some companies will offer new issues, but only if the investor also buys warrants. This combination is called a unit. Typically a unit might be one stock and one warrant.

The advantage to the company of issuing units is that not only does it get the revenue from the stock issue, but it also gets the revenue from the warrants. Yet, it does not have to issue any stock for the warrants until some time in the future. If the stock value doesn't hold up or drops, the warrants will become worthless and no investors will exercise them; hence the company *may never* have to issue stock for them. Money taken in by a company for warrants can, thus, be pure gravy.

## AFTERMARKET REQUIRED PURCHASES

Some brokers will sell you new issues only if you agree to buy an equal number of shares of the same stock in the aftermarket. This is the broker's way of insuring that you

## WEALTH BUILDERS

aren't going to speculate, buy, and then dump the new issue.

There's no advantage I can see to the investor in such an arrangement. Quite the contrary, there's considerable disadvantage. If the stock shoots up, you're committed to buying at the higher price. If it drops, you're commited to buying a stock that could quickly become worthless.

When possible, the best advice is to stay away from brokers who insist on this arrangement. (It usually crops up only when the market is hot.)

### BLUE-SKY LAWS

Depending on the state in which you live, you may or may not be able to buy new issues. Many of the states in the country have restrictive laws with regard to them.

These restrictive laws (called blue-sky laws) are in the form of regulation of new issues in addition to the SEC regulation at the national level.

The basic difference between blue-sky regulation and SEC regulation has to do with merit versus disclosure. The SEC requires full disclosure only in a prospectus. However, some states insist that in addition, the state pass a merit judgment on the stock (judge whether or not it's a good and safe investment).

"That sounds like a good idea," said Gail.

It would be, I replied, if the state's criteria for merit was standardized and reasonable. However, each state with blue-sky laws has different standards and some are outrageous. For a new small company to seek approval in all these various states would cost a fortune, would take many years, and, in some cases, would prove impossible.

# THE PENNY STOCK BOOM

"If I live in one of those states I can't buy new issues?" Gail looked quite disappointed.

What it means, I replied, is that a broker can't sell you stock if your residence is in that state. Some enterprising investors, however, maintain a residence in a clear state and purchase the stock from there. Other investors have relatives or friends in clear states make the purchase instead of them.

## GETTING STARTED

"I feel like I'm ready to roll!" said Gail.

I smiled, but cautioned her. We've really only scratched the surface I said. There's a lot more to be understood about penny stocks.

"Are there any good books I can read?" she asked.

I've been searching for a good book on penny stocks myself for several years, I replied, but haven't found any I could recommend. I advise you to ease yourself into the market. Test the waters to see what feels right, then try it. Invest only small amounts until you learn enough to be comfortable.

And be sure to write out exactly what you plan to do. Write down that you plan to invest no more than, for example, $1,500 over the next six months or year. Write down that you're going to spend $500 in new issues and $1,000 in aftermarket or whatever. Write down what profit you'll accept before you sell.

Penny stocks represent an almost unique opportunity in America today. They offer a way to get in on the ground floor of thousands of new companies, some of which will be the giants of tomorrow.

# CONCLUSION

We have now looked at six different investment areas, any of which could be your road to riches. (I was talking for the last time to the Future Millionaires' Investment Club.) However, before tackling any of them, it's important to remember that we are living in an era when the only constant is constant change.

By the time you read this, some entirely new investment may have cropped up that appears to be wonderful. If that's the case, examine it carefully. How does it fit in with what you now know about the influence of liquidity (interest rates [borrowing] and inflation) on our times?

Even more so, when considering an investment, I urge you to remember the perspectives with which we began. You'll recall there were seven Loser's Reasonings to avoid. Here they are again, this time restated as seven *don'ts*:

1. Don't rely on just positive thinking. (It helps, but you need real knowledge as well to succeed.)
2. Don't follow the financial hero of the moment.
3. Don't try to duplicate someone else's investment success.
4. Don't get burned by "hot" investments.

## CONCLUSION

5. Don't wait too long to invest.
6. Don't worry about losing some money.
7. Don't trust a seller.

Of course the biggest *don't* to remember is, *Don't blame someone else for your investment mistakes.* If we're ready to claim credit for any success we have, then we must also be responsible for any investment setbacks that we run into. It's not the president or the Federal Reserve Board or the Trilateral Commission or our husband or wife that messed up; it's us. Once we recognize this, we can move forward to success.

We should also remember the four keys to achieving that investment success that we desire:

1. Make your own luck.
2. Pay your dues.
3. Move with the times.
4. Have a plan written out.

Finally, it's important to remember that there are no guarantees in this life. Some of you (I hope, most) will go on to great investment success. Others won't. There's nothing that I've said or written that in any way guarantees or assures your success. You might win, but you might also lose.

The best that any of us can hope for is to give our investing an honest try. The worst is to sit back, watch someone else succeed, and say to ourselves, "I could have done that, if only . . ."

# INDEX

Adjustable-rate mortgages (ARMs), 65, 75–76
Aftermarket, 174, 175, 181–182
American Numismatic Association, 118
ANACS, 124
American Stock Exchange, 174
Appreciation, 40, 51
Ask price, 180
Astor, John Jacob, 39

Baby-boom demand for housing, 47
Barnum, P. T., 18
Bid price, 180
Blue-sky laws, 196–197
Bonds, 3
Bullion, defined, 84
Buy downs, 64–65

Caesar, Julius, 28
Calls, 137–142
Camus, Albert, 28
Canadian maple leaf, 108
Churchill, Winston, 28
Commodities futures market, 109–110, 135–136
Coins, 13, 37, 107–108, 114–133
    anticipation, role of, 130–131
    certificates, 124
    counterfeits and sliders, 125–126
    dealers, 122–123
    gold, 107–108, 132
    grading, 118–123
    inflation and, 130
    interest rates and, 130–131
    rules for buying and selling, 126–130
    what to buy, 131–132
Counterfeit coins, 125–126
Creative financing, 56, 66, 67, 73

Depreciation, 32, 79–80
Down payments, 66–67
Dues paying, 23–25, 199

Fear of losing, 17
Federal deficit, 34–35
Federal Reserve Bank, 33, 34
FHA loans, 67
50-peso, 107, 108
Financial heroes, 10–12, 198
Financial statement, 160–161
Fixed-rate mortgages, 65, 75–77
Fixer-upper market, 70–75
Foreign currency, 26
Futures contracts, 26

Gold, 4–5, 19, 26, 37, 83–87, 102–103
    coins, 107–108, 132
    inflation and, 86–89
    interest rates and, 87–88
    jewelry demand and, 90–92
    market manipulation, 95
    oil connection and, 89–90

# INDEX

Gold (continued)
    paper, 109–110
    ratio to silver, 99, 102
    rules for buying, 104–108
    supply of, 92–93
    timing in buying, 93–94
    world crisis and, 85–86, 88, 89
Grading coins, 118–123

Hidden knowledge, 11
High-tech stocks, 184–185
House price, 52, 55–56

Inactive investors, 49, 50
Inflation, 32, 33, 36
    coins and, 130
    gold and, 86–89
    real estate and, 45–46, 62
Interest deduction, 80
Interest rates, 33, 35–36
    coins and, 130–131
    gold and, 87–88
    real estate and, 44–46, 62, 64–65, 76–77
Intrinsic value, 139–140, 144

Jewelry, 90–92

Kennedy, John F., 28
Krugerrands, 107–108, 132

Leveraged buying, 110
Liquidity, 34, 35–36, 130
Location, real estate investing and, 68–70
Loser's Reasonings, 9–20, 198–199
Losing, fear of, 17
Luck, 21–23, 57, 199

Market makers, 176, 178–179
Millionaires, number of, 7
Mingling, 53–54, 68, 69
Mining stocks, 184
Money market funds, 5

Mortgages, 44–46, 51, 59, 64–65, 67, 75–79
Moving with times, 25–27, 199

NASDAQ (National Association of Securities Dealers Automated Quotations), 179
National debt, 34–35
Neighborhood growth, 61–63
New homes, 55–56, 60–61, 63–66
New issues, 174, 175, 187–197
New York Stock Exchange, 176
Nothing-downers, 3–4, 39, 43, 48

Oil, 89–90
Options, 26, 37, 110, 136–148
    real estate, 136–137
    stock, 137–148
Over-the-counter (OTC) market, 176–177, 181

Palladium, 83, 111–112
PAMs (partially amortized mortgages), 67
Paper gold and silver, 109–110
Paper leveraging, 110
Passive investors, 49
Penny stocks, 37, 147, 168–197
    aftermarket, profiting from, 181–182
    buying, 179–180
    defined, 170
    new issues, 174, 175, 187–197
    prospectus, 192–194
    sources of information on, 185–186
    timing in buying, 186–187
    what to buy, 183–185
Perfect investments, waiting for, 15–16
Persistence, 17
Platinum, 83, 111–112
Players, 17–18
PMI loans, 66
Poker, 22, 166

## INDEX

Positive thinking, 9–10, 198
Productivity, 33, 34
Promotional companies, 185
Prospectus, 192–194
Puts, 138, 143–145
Pyramid games, 12–13

Real estate, 3–4, 8, 32, 33, 37–81
    financing, 56, 63–67, 75–79
    fixer-upper method, 70–75
    holding homes long-term, 49–56
    house price, 52, 55–56
    inflation and, 45–46, 62
    interest rates and, 44–46, 62, 64–65, 76–77
    location, 68–70
    neighborhood growth, 61–63
    new homes, 55–56, 60–61, 63–66
    options, 136–137
    rental market, 52–55, 67–68
    taxes and, 32, 51, 59, 79–80
    yesterday's rules, 40–42
Rent control, 54
Rental market, 52–55, 67–68
Risk, 2

Securities Exchange Commission (SEC), 177, 192
Sellers, questioning motives of, 18–20
Silver, 14–15, 26, 37, 95
    futures market and, 97–98
    medium-term investment in, 98–99
    paper, 109–110
    ratio to gold, 99, 102
    rules for buying, 104–109
    volatility of, 96–97

Silver bars, 108
Silver dollars, 108
Skill, 29
Sliders, 125–126
Spread, 148, 180
Stock exchanges, 176–177
Stock options, 137–148
Stocks, 5, 26, 31–32
    *See also* Penny stocks
Straddles, 145–146
Studying investments, 13–15
Success, four keys to, 21–29, 199

Taxes, real estate investing and, 32, 51, 59, 79–80
Tax sales, 37, 150–167
    attending, 164–167
    drawbacks of, 155–157
    lots purchased at, 158–161
    preparation for, 163–164
    reasons for, 153–154
    sources of information on, 162–163
Timing, 16, 26, 28, 199
$20 double eagles, 108, 132

Underwriters, 178, 190
Units, 195

Venture-capital market, 172–173
Volatility, 140–141, 144, 147

Warrants, 194–195
World crisis, gold and the, 85–86, 88, 89
Written plan, 27–29, 112, 133, 148, 167, 199